Tippu Tip
and the East African Slave Trade

LEDA FARRANT

Tippu Tip
and the East African
Slave Trade

ST. MARTIN'S PRESS
NEW YORK

DEDICATION

My gratitude for their help and encouragement
goes to Juan, Robert and Gary, my parents, Sheila
and Joe Murumbi and Jamie Hamilton

Contents

v

Illustrations

Between pages 84 and 85

Tippu Tip's Family Tree

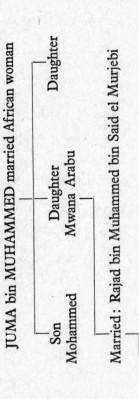

JUMA bin MUHAMMED married African woman

Son Mohammed   Daughter Mwana Arabu   Daughter

Married: Rajad bin Muhammed bin Said el Murjebi

Juma bin Rajad (Tippu Tip's grandfather)

Muhammed bin Juma (Tippu Tip's father)

Married: In Tabora: KARUNDE, Chief Fundikira's daughter.

In Zanzibar: Bint Habib bin Bushir (Tippu Tip's mother)

Hamed bin Muhammed (Tippu Tip)

Introduction

Hamed bin Muhammed bin Juma bin Rajad el Murjebi better known as Tippu Tip, was one of the last great slavers of the 19th century. His rule extended for thousands of miles, west and north west of Lake Tanganyika, and his name was known and feared in most of East and Central Africa. Great explorers such as Livingstone, Cameron, Stanley and Wismann knew him well and made extensive use of his power over the African tribes and his intimate knowledge of the regions they explored. Leopold, King of the Belgians, appointed him Governor of the Congo Free State, and the Sultan of Zanzibar wanted to appoint him Wali (Governor) of Tabora: the important stronghold of Zanzibar Arabs in Central Tanganyika.

Despite the fact that every white man Tippu Tip met knew he traded in human flesh with terrible results for the victims, they all admired him as a man of great character, courage and strength.

When Stanley first met him on the Lualaba River (west of Lake Tanganyika) in October 1876, he wrote about Tippu Tip. [1] 'He was a tall black-bearded man, of negroid complexion, in the prime of life, straight, and quick in his movements, a picture of energy and strength. He had a fine intelligent face, with a nevous twitching of the eyes, and gleaming white and perfectly-formed teeth. He was attended by a large retinue of young Arabs, who looked up to him as chief, and a score of Wangwana and Wanyamwezi followers whom he had led over thousands of miles through Africa. With the air of a well-bred Arab, and almost courtier-like in his manner, he welcomed me to Mwana Mamba's village, and his slaves being ready at hand with mat and bolster, he reclined vis-à-vis, while a buzz of admiration of his

[1] Henry Morton Stanley's *Through the Dark Continent*, 1879.

ix

style was perceptible from the on-lookers. After regarding him for a few minutes, I came to the conclusion that this Arab was a remarkable man—the most remarkable man I had met among Arabs, Wa-Swahili, and half-castes of Africa. He was neat in his person, his clothes were of a spotless white, his fez-cap brand-new, his waist was encircled by a rich dowle, his dagger was splendid with silver filigree, and his *tout ensemble* was that of an Arab gentleman in very comfortable circumstances.'

Stanley was anxious to enlist Tippu Tip's help in his search for the Congo River but the frightening stories told by one of Tippu Tip's followers about the never ending 'wall of trees' between them and the river which the explorer believed to be the Congo, made it all seem an impossible undertaking.

'And are you still prepared to follow me?' Stanley asked his host when Tippu Tip's man had finished his tale of horror and death.

'I think with my help and your guns we can get through.'

'He had resolved to accompany me a distance of sixty camps,' Stanley wrote. 'Each camp to be four hours march from the other, for the sum of five thousand dollars.' Tippu Tip, on the other hand, says that he was offered seven thousand dollars. 'Of course the money was not important to me,' he told Professor Brode many years later. [2] 'I didn't need the money, but the man asked for my help and I agreed to help him.'

To convince the explorer that he was not a man looking for employment, he showed him his enormous stores of ivory, and Stanley was duly impressed, but not as impressed as Tippu Tip with Stanley's guns.

'This gun can shoot fifteen times in a row,' Stanley said showing him a 'repeating gun'.

'All out of one barrel?' Tippu Tip was sceptical.

'All out of one barrel.' Stanley replied.

'I have never seen nor heard of such a gun,' Tippu Tip said turning the shining weapon in his hands. 'Show me how it works.'

'I am sorry. Ammunition is too precious to waste on games,' Stanley replied impatiently.

Tippu Tip smiled politely at the obvious lie, and after a while he said: 'I have a bow which takes twenty arrows. When you

[2] Heinrich Brode's *Tippu Tip*, 1903.

fire, all twenty arrows fly together and each arrow kills a man. I am sorry I cannot show it to you.'[3]

This was too much for Stanley. He snatched the gun from Tippu Tip's hands and fired twelve rounds, then he took a pistol and fired six rounds. 'The Arab was convinced. He asked to examine the gun and be shown how to load it.'

After these demonstrations of wealth and power, Tippu Tip signed the agreement and prepared to escort the explorer into the unknown.

His vanity would have been flattered by Stanley's description of their first meeting, but for one detail: the mention of his negroid complexion. Tippu Tip was very touchy on this subject. He considered himself a pure Arab and the fact that anybody should notice that his complexion and features betrayed some African blood, annoyed him intensely. In fact, he inherited his negroid features from an African great-great-grandmother.

Hamed bin Muhammed, later nicknamed Tippu Tip, was therefore almost justified in considering himself a full blooded Arab gentleman, despite his negroid features. He certainly behaved like an Arab, but he was perhaps a little more insistent in demanding respect from all who met him, than the average Arab trader. His narrative is frequently peppered with the words: 'They treated me with great respect',[4] and one soon gets the impression that this powerful man suffered from at least one inferiority complex, which perhaps explains his wish to be recognised as the benefactor of all the explorers who passed through his territories. In those days an Arab would consider it a great slight to be mistaken for an African.

Hamed bin Muhammed was also very conscious of the nervous twitching of his eyes, and although he was known as 'the one who blinks', or Tippu Tip, he didn't like that interpretation of his nickname. As he told the German Professor Heinrich Brode in 1903 when the latter recorded Tippu Tip's life in Swahili and then published it in German, 'the name Tippu Tip had been given me by the locals who had fled to Urungu. They said they had seen many Wangwana[5] and had seized their goods but this

[3] *Maisha ya Hamed bin Muhammed el Murjebi, yaani Tippu Tip.* Edited by Prof. Brode.
[4] *Maisha ya Hamed bin Muhammed el Murjebi, yaani Tippu Tip.*
[5] Wangwana: freemen of Zanzibar.

man's guns went tiptip in a manner too terrible to listen to. That was how I got my name Tip Tip.'[6]

On the other hand, Livingstone writes that, 'the sheik (Tippu Tip) at the sight of Nsama's[7] treasures, exclaimed: now I am Tippoo Tib, the gatherer of wealth.'[8] [9]

Tippu Tip was very fond of these latter versions. He was very vain, and never more so than when in the presence of a European. He always enjoyed showing off to Stanley for instance, as Stanley was somewhat vain and boastful himself.

Today, Tippu Tip cannot be regarded as a hero since his exploits and gains were at the expense of other human beings. He must, however, be regarded as a brave and daring adventurer, a good administrator, and a great leader of men. He also opened up unknown parts of Africa and helped the explorers who described them to the world. When he died, a small item in *The Times* announced the death of one of the greatest slavers, but not a word about the part he played in the discovery of the African interior, the help and protection he gave explorers and missionaries, and the fact that in doing so he brought about the end of slavery, Arab domination and his own destruction in the very countries which he conquered and held for almost thirty years.

Whatever else he was, Tippu Tip was certainly one of the most colourful and adventurous characters Africa produced during an era when there was an overabundance of colourful and adventurous characters.

[6] Tippu Tip's name was spelt in many different ways by the Europeans who wrote about him. I have adopted the spelling used in Tippu Tip's own memoirs as dictated to Heinrich Brode.

[7] Nsama: Chief Samu of Itawa whom Tippu Tip fought and defeated.

[8] From David Livingstone's *Last Journals.*

[9] Tippu Tip spoke perfect Arabic and Kiswahili. He also spoke some of the tribal languages, but very little English.

CHAPTER ONE

Zanzibar

Approached from the sea the island of Zanzibar is one of the most beautiful sights in the world. It was so in the 1830s when Tippu Tip was born there, and it is still so today. The island certainly deserves to be known as the Green Jewel of the Indian Ocean—at a distance.

Thirty miles of water, from the deepest blues to the clearest greens, separate the island from the African mainland, the sea gently lapping against the sandy beaches and the coral coves. As the boat approaches, the lush green of the island comes into view. The fringed leaves of the stately coco-nut palms wave gently in the breeze against a deep blue sky, the enormous dark green mango trees are everywhere, and at certain times of the year, there is a delicate fragrance of spices in the air. [1] Two and three storey white buildings, mosques and minarets shimmer in the sun like a mirage. Even in the 1830s some of them were palatial buildings, and the most palatial of all, the Sultan's palace, flew the red flag of its ruler. Although no European nation was formally represented in Zanzibar until later, many flags were in evidence as one approached the island in those days. British, French, German, Portuguese, Dutch and even American frigates and steam-ships were anchored alongside the dozens of colourful Arab dhows. Zanzibar was the most strategic and important port along the East African coast, and no man knew this better than Seyyid Said, the Sultan who ruled when Tippu Tip was born.

The romantic, whether he was an explorer, a representative of his government, an adventurer or a missionary (and some of the white men who went to Zanzibar in those days, were often

---

[1] A number of spices grow wild in Zanzibar, but the clove plantations were developed by Sultan Said in 1840.

all of these things), soon realised that the Green Jewel they so admired from the sea presented another face altogether on closer inspection.

The palms and the mango trees, the Sultan's palace, the white buildings and the mosques were still there; but behind this façade were narrow, hot, stinking alleyways where petty merchants lived and traded. The narrow back streets of Zanzibar were populated by the poorer Swahilis, Arabs, Comorians, Baluchis, Indians and their slaves. Their small houses were joined to one another, built of coral and lime and entered through sometimes beautifully carved doors. The centre of the house was the courtyard with perhaps one or two paw-paw trees growing in it, and always chickens and children squawking on the hard earthen floor. The rooms of the house were built around and opening onto the courtyard. The size of the house depended on the merchant's varying degree of success. Most of the women were kept in strict purdah, unless they were non-Muslim slaves, and when they ventured out into the streets, they were covered from head to toe in the black Buibui, which is the hottest kind of black cover-all that any woman could choose to please her lord and master.

The filth of these houses flowed through open drains by the side of the dark alleyways, down to the great receptacle—the green blue sea. David Livingstone referred to Zanzibar as *Stinkibar*. 'The stench arising from a mile and a half of the filth of the town, is quite horrible. At night it is so gross and crass one might cut out a slice and manure a garden with it. No-one long enjoys good health here.' [2]

One baby who was enjoying very good health there was Tippu Tip. His name was still Hamed bin Muhammed then and he belonged to the privileged or 'upper class' of Zanzibaris. The meaning of upper class in Zanzibar in the 1830s was not exactly what was meant by 'upper class' in Victorian England for example. Nothing to do with Public Schools or Clubs. Upper class meant that you were an Arab first and foremost, that your family could afford plantations and town houses *and* a great number of slaves. Slaves were *heshima*. [3]

Little Hamed was born with all these privileges as his father enjoyed a thriving business in ivory and slaves. The fact that his

[2] David Livingstone's *Last Journals*.
[3] A Swahili word meaning Honour, Prestige.

great-great-grandmother had been an African, had little bearing on his family's claim, and later his own claim, that he was a full-blooded Arab.

Nevertheless, Hamed's full-blooded Arab mother, Bint Habib bin Bushir, looked at her infant son and wondered. 'How could a son of mine be so dark?' She said to the women of her family surrounding her. [4] Baby Hamed was almost as black as the African slave women who attended to her needs in that hot stuffy room at Kwarara where she had just given birth to the first Arab son of the trader to whom she had been married a year before. When Hamed was born her husband was 500 miles away in Tabora, his major inland depot. Bint Habib knew that he had concubines and an African wife there. That was natural. A man had to have his comforts, but Hamed was his first *Arab* son and heir. [5] What would Muhammed say when he found that his Arab son looked so African? His nose was large and flat and his lips seemed enormous as he sucked ravenously at his mother's breast. Bint Habib would soon find out. Although messages could take two or three months, or forever, to reach Tabora, Muhammed would not be long in returning to sell his ivory and slaves.

The one thing all the inhabitants of Zanzibar had in common was slavery. Even the miserable dwellers of the back streets had a few slaves, and sometimes the slaves had slaves of their own. The whole economy of this lush and smelly island revolved around

[4] From unpublished Letters and Private Papers belonging to the Murjebi family. Throughout the book these references will be marked as 'Murjebi Family Papers'.

[5] No prestige was lost in having black concubines. Quite the contrary. Sultan Said was reputed to have had 70 in his harem, and three Arab wives. From all these women he had 112 children and according to Mohammedan law, the children, whether born of legal wives or concubines, were all legitimate and the sons could become heirs to their father's throne. Only thirty-six children were still living by the time Sultan Said died. Enough to create quite an inheritance problem, but one of the daughters, the Princess Salme never got a penny, rupee or Deutsch Mark despite the international legal bargaining that went on for many years after her father's death. Princess Salme was said to be very beautiful and as her house was next door to the offices of a German company (Oswald & Co.), she was often observed and admired by a lonely German bachelor employed there. Eventually they eloped together. A dreadful sin for a Mohammedan princess. Had it not been for the help of a British warship which carried the lovers to Aden, they would have never survived in Zanzibar where the Sultan would have executed them both.

3

the trade. The slaves were needed for the local plantations, but most of all for export. Zanzibar was the most important slave market in the Indian Ocean. Ivory was a most important commodity, but without slave porters it could have never reached the Zanzibar market.

Hamed bin Muhammed's father, and his grandfather before him, dealt in these commodities and the slave business was thriving throughout the Sultan's territories despite British efforts, threats and promises.

The powerful and astute Sultan entertained the British representative, Colonel Hamerton, over sherbert, sweetmeats and coffee. They were great friends, and respected each other. The Sultan wanted British assistance in Muscat, where the other half of his subjects were always giving trouble and he also wanted the British to prevent the French from grabbing his beautiful and profitable Zanzibar. In exchange the British wanted the Sultan to stop his subjects trading in slaves.

The slow and friendly negotiations between the Sultan and Colonel Hamerton went on for many years and meanwhile Hamed grew fat and strong at Kwarara, a plantation belonging to his mother's family near the town of Zanzibar and away from the unhealthy atmosphere of that town. The plantation was not a large one but there were plenty of coconuts, which were delicious shredded on rice cooked in the coconut milk, and also good for curries and sweet cakes. A coconut tree, which takes seven or eight years to bear fruit and lives for fifty years or more, is one of the most useful trees in the world. Besides its food value, floor matting, roof coverings and ropes are made from its branches, oil is extracted from it and even kitchen ladles can be made out of the shells, and when its uses are exhausted, it makes very good fuel. Besides the useful coconut palms, sweet and bitter cassava and of course paw-paws, bananas, mangoes, oranges and limes were grown. The heat and the humidity were intense for so many months of the year that a lazy, soporific atmosphere pervaded the whole island, but like their gardens, the Arabs flourished naturally and without effort. Only the Europeans, in their tightly buttoned-up uniforms and inhibiting morality, suffered from frustrations and prickly-heat.

One of the British 'frustrations' had just landed at the busy and congested port of Zanzibar. A few feet away from the British Consulate, Muhammed bin Juma, Hamed's father, was busy arranging for the unloading of the dhows which had ferried his ivory and slaves from the mainland. Everything had to be passed through the Sultan's Custom's House, a sizeable building, hot and dirty but efficiently run by an Indian who made sure that for every slave imported into Zanzibar the Sultan received the equivalent of one pound sterling. The business would take hours, sometimes days, but the slaves were securely locked up in 'pens', therefore there was no hurry. Only the Europeans hurried and died young in Zanzibar. Muhammed bin Juma had personal business to attend to at Kwarara.

Hamed was over a year old when he first met his father. 'He's a handsome boy,' Muhammed said to his anxious wife. 'He's strong and clever,' he went on as little Hamed tugged at the silver dagger strapped to his father's waist. 'Look at him. He's not afraid of anything. Already he walks and talks better than any of his cousins.'[5]

The household at Kwarara was typical of many other Arab households in Zanzibar. Swarming with children of all ages, dressed in the white *lungi*[6] and little embroidered white caps; Arab women in long dresses and white pantaloons frilled at the ankles; Swahili women wrapped in colourful kangas,[7] and slaves in the castoffs of their masters. The slaves did everything. They cultivated the plantations, took care of the children, cooked, cleaned and pampered the women. An elderly and trusted slave was in charge, an eunuch who had been with the family since he was born. He saw that everything ran smoothly and was responsible to the master for the protection of the women and the punishment of offending slaves. The women, both legal wives and concubines, all lived in the same house but in different quarters and away from their husbands, unless called to duty. They gossiped and quarrelled and schemed to obtain extra favours for themselves and their children, but when the master arrived, all was peace—at least on the surface. The luxury of the individual members of the harem depended on her husband's wealth and favour. On this occasion, Bint Habib bin Bushir, was in great favour. She was young, handsome, Arab and had given her husband what was expected of her, a son. Therefore she

[5] Murjebi Family Papers.
[6] Long white gowns sometimes called Kanzu.
[7] Two yards of colourfully printed cotton used as a sarong by Swahili women.

5

commanded respect and special treatment from the rest of the household and was well pleased with herself. There was no question as to who would share her husband's chamber during his stay in Zanzibar.

Looking after a man, his house and his children was a woman's work, but Muhammed had come to Zanzibar for more reasons than meeting his son and enjoying his wife. There was business to attend to. The slaves and the ivory had to be sold and another caravan assembled to carry supplies, ammunition and goods for barter back to Tabora.

Muhammed made his way to the Changani slave market to supervise the last arrangements before the afternoon sale started. Everybody greeted and congratulated him as he strode through the dusty streets swinging his walking cane. There was always an air of excitement in Zanzibar when a trader came back with a good stock of ivory and slaves, and for the occasion Muhammed wore his best silver dagger and gold embroidered waistcoat over the white *lungi*.

The market square was already crowded when he arrived. Dhow captains, local buyers and idle spectators examining the goods and waiting for the sale to start. Muhammed's own slaves were leading the slaves for sale to the cages in which they would be sold. Muhammed was a wholesaler, therefore he sold slaves in lots, not individually.

Each cage was about twenty feet square and it could hold up to 150 slaves. This time he had brought 600 men, women and children for sale and as he walked slowly around them, he decided how many of each would go to make up a cage. As a rule a cage contained a mixed group of varying ages, physical condition, health and strength, but Muhammed was careful in his choice. Too many or too few of one kind could mean the difference between a large and small profit. He never separated the women from their infants, but he separated husbands and wives as the buyers found them troublesome together and didn't pay as much for couples.

A few young and handsome girls he sold separately as the retailers would resell them as concubines and greater profits could be made. These girls received very special attention. Whereas the slaves in cages were washed and greased with coconut oil to make their bodies shine and give them a healthy glow, the girls were also painted and wrapped in colourful *kangas*. Outstanding girls were given gold ear and nose rings, bracelets and anklets, but these were of course removed after the sale. Muhammed expected to get between ten and fifteen pounds for each girl this time. A young healthy girl represented good 'reproducing' value to her master, as any of her off-spring became his property automatically. Very often the girl became the Arab's concubine and then any child she conceived was born a 'freeman'.

Richard Burton wrote that 'the domestic slave-girl rarely has issue. The chief cause is that the captive has no interest in becoming a mother (as) her progeny by another slave may be sold away from her at any moment and she obviates the pains and penalties of maternity by the easy process of procuring abortions. The Muwallid (the slave born in the family), belongs solely to his mother's owner, who sells him or gives him away at pleasure. One born a slave is a slave for ever, even in the next world,' he said. [8]

Little boys were also sold for great profits and Muhammed selected twenty of them to be auctioned separately. For the past three months, as they travelled from Tabora, he had taken special care of these boys. Eunuchs were always in great demand all over the Arab world and a boy had to be healthy to survive castration. Muhammed had nothing to do with the operation. It was done in Zanzibar after he had sold the boys to retailers or wherever the new owners took them. The operation was not always successful and if the child didn't die under the knife, he was abandoned to die crawling around the filthy streets begging for food and help. Even a hardened slaver like Muhammed was revolted by the sight.

In general children fetched a very good price as they were quick to learn their masters' ways and gave no trouble. They were also used for homosexual purposes as the Arabs considered the practice perfectly normal, and a heterosexual was not frowned upon for having male partners. Some of the women practised homosexuality in the harems where life without men could become rather boring, and again, this was not disapproved of, but it was certainly not practised as openly as by the men.

Muhammed hated the crying of the children and the screaming of their mothers when they were separated, therefore he tried to select the future eunuchs from boys who had no parents. These had been bought and sold so many times before that they

[8] R. F. Burton's *Zanzibar*, 1872.

hardly noticed another change of masters. The rest he used to balance out a 'bad lot' in one cage. There was no room for humanitarian feelings in this trade and no man could make a profit by being humane; besides which very few slaves were strong enough to care after months of marching and starving. They only moved when prodded or whipped, otherwise they stood or squatted apathetically waiting to be sold to the next master.

The next master would take them to the markets of Arabia, Muscat, Persia, Turkey or Egypt, but quite a number of Muhammed's customers were local retailers who sold the slaves as and when they could. The best time was of course when the dhows arrived from Aden and the Persian Gulf.

The first Englishman to report on the Zanzibar slave trade was Captain Smee. [9] The British Indian government had sent him to the East African coast on a 'voyage of research' in 1811 and this is how he describes the retailers' methods of sale.... 'The slaves are ranged in a line commencing with the youngest and increasing to the rear according to their size and age. At the head of this file, which is composed of all sexes and ages from six to sixty, walks the person who owns them. Behind and at each side two or three of his domestic slaves, armed with swords and spears, serve as guards. Thus ordered, the procession begins and passes through the market-place and principal streets, the owner holding forth in a kind of song the good qualities of his slaves and the high prices that have been offered for them. When any of them strikes a spectator's fancy, the line immediately stops, and a process of examination ensues which for minuteness is unequalled in any cattle-market in Europe. The intending purchaser, having ascertained there is no defect in the faculties of speech, hearing, etc., that there is no disease present, and that the slave does not snore in sleeping which is counted a very great fault, next proceeds to examine the person: the mouth and the teeth are first inspected, and afterwards every part of the body in succession, not even excepting the breasts etc. of the girls, many of whom I have seen handled in the most indecent manner in the public market by their purchasers: indeed there is every reason to believe that the slave-dealers almost universally force the young females to submit to their lust previous to their being disposed of. The slave is then made to walk or run a little way

[9] Captain Thomas Smee of the ship *Ternate*.

8

to show there is no defect about the feet; after which if the price is agreed to, they are stripped of their finery and delivered over to their future master ... Women and children newly born hanging at their breasts and others so old they scarcely walk, are sometimes seen dragged about in this manner. I observed they had in general a very dejected look; some groups appeared so ill fed that their bones appeared as if ready to penetrate the skin. ...'

Other accounts of the Zanzibar market, thirty, forty and fifty years later, all read like a continuation of Captain Smee's report, and were all equally indignant. Perhaps the 'Zanzibar Smithfield', as Captain Devereux [10] describes the slave market, was too close a reminder of the part England played on the West coast of Africa; anyway there was nothing shocking in the sale of slaves as far as Muhammed or his countrymen were concerned. It was a trade like any other trade. A slave was no more than a piece of merchandise which had to be sold at the best price possible, and besides the blacks were 'washenzi' to an Arab. Pagans without a soul. Uncivilised beings of a lower order. Perhaps later, when they had been bought and lived with a family for some years, they might be regarded as people, but on the market they were merchandise to the Arabs, and Muhammed was well satisfied with the prices his merchandise was fetching that day.

[10] W. C. Devereux *A Cruise in the Gordon*, 1869.

CHAPTER TWO

Hamed's Training

When he was six years old Hamed was sent to a teacher of the Koran to learn to read and write and like all the other little boys in Zanzibar he sat cross-legged in the mosque repeating passages from the Koran and getting swatted over the head by the teacher when he forgot his lines.

He also helped in his mother's shamba [1] but he found all this very dull work for a man. His greatest wish and ambition was to join his father and his trading caravans. He day-dreamed of fighting great armies of savage warriors and making them all his prisoners, then returning to be rewarded by the Sultan and feasted by the people of Zanzibar. He sometimes acted out these dreams with his friends, but by the time he was twelve he wanted more than play-acting and living with women. His uncle, Bushiri bin Hamid traded in gum-copal and finally Hamed and his brother Muhamed bin Masud el Wardi, were allowed to join him on his trading expeditions to the mainland. A small beginning for such an ambitious child, but better than repeating the Koran in the mosque or listening to women's gossip.

Gum-copal was not as exciting as slaves or even ivory, but there was a feeling of adventure in sailing the dhows back and forth to the mainland. Especially now that the British cruisers patrolled the Oceans. Their small dhow was often stopped and searched for illegal slaves by the crew of the British boats, and little Hamed, squatting on smelly bags of copal, watched the British sailors as they checked the dhow's papers and learnt more than he had ever learnt in the mosque.

In 1845, when Hamed was still learning the Koran, Sultan Said had signed a 'ratification' of the 'Moresby Treaty' for the

[1] Swahili for garden, vegetable garden, plantation or farm.

suppression of the export of slaves outside his East African dominions. This meant that the Arabs of Zanzibar and on the mainland were still allowed to buy and sell slaves, but not to export them to other countries. The Sultan also agreed to the British navy sending cruisers to patrol the East African waters to ensure that no dhow broke the law. As Hamed's father and his fellow slavers became richer and richer, one can imagine how successful the navy and the treaties were. Of course, the treaty created a problem, especially as Seyyid[2] Said wanted to keep the British happy and co-operate in his struggle against his subjects in Muscat and the French intrigues in Zanzibar; but the smuggling of slaves from his territories was happily carried out by his subjects and he happily accepted their tax dues.

Slavery had been declared illegal in Britain in 1807, and through the efforts of political philanthropists like William Wilberforce (1759-1833), and later Thomas Fowell Buxton (1786-1845), it was finally suppressed in the British colonies.

Zanzibar was not a British colony, but under British influence after Seyyid Said invited the British government to appoint a consul there. This invitation brought a number of advantages but also a lot of disadvantages for all involved in the slave trade. The island traders, the Indian bankers, the dhow captains, the market retailers and finally the Sultan, were all affected by this sudden British effort to stamp out slave trading in the Indian Ocean. After a mere signature on a treaty and the promise of a few rewards, they were all expected to give up their age-old way of life and enormous profits. From the moment the British Consul, Captain Hamerton, set foot in Zanzibar, the anti-slavery pressure was applied and never relinquished. British consul succeeded British consul, and Sultan succeeded Sultan, but the pressure increased. Some consuls were more successful than others. Captain Hamerton during the reign of Seyyid Said,[3] Colonel Rigby at the time of Seyyid Majid,[4] and Dr. Kirk with Seyyid Barghash,[5] were vital figures during a period when the British were determined to force the Sultans to abandon slave trading, and the Arabs were equally determined to maintain Zanzibar as it had been long before British consuls were appointed: the most lucrative market in the Indian Ocean.

At his age Hamed didn't understand the political significance

[2] Seyyid and Sultan have the same meaning.
[3] 1841-1858, [4] 1856-1870, [5] 1870-1888.

11

of the British cruisers, but he immediately accepted the need for secrecy. His uncle didn't transport slaves, his dhow was not fitted out for that trade, but sometimes he did hide a few slaves under the sacks of copal to do a friend a favour. Hamed was learning very fast. Both in Zanzibar and on the mainland at Kilwa and Bagamoyo, his father's friends allowed him to visit the customs' house, the slave dhows and barracoons [6] where the slaves were 'stored' waiting to be loaded on dhows. He could walk anywhere, everybody knew he was Muhammed bin Juma's son. He noticed that the dhows used for the short crossing between the mainland ports and Zanzibar, known as the 'middle passage', [7] were smaller than the ocean-going dhows which operated between Arabia and East Africa, but the method of *stowing* was very much the same on both types of vessels. Temporary platforms of bamboo were built, leaving a narrow passage in the centre. The slaves were then stowed in bulk. The first on the floor of the boat, two adults side by side, with a boy or a girl resting between or on them, until the tier was complete. Over them the first platform was laid an inch or two above their bodies, where a second tier was stowed, and so on until the boat was filled.

Depending on the weather and the interference of British cruisers, the dhows took two or three days for the crossing. During that period the slaves were given the minimum of food and water, and if the passage took longer than expected, they quietly died and were thrown overboard when the owners of the dhows came to unload.

Between the time of unloading and selling on the market, if a slave looked as if he might not survive the interim period, he was thrown overboard anyway, to avoid paying the customs' duty. This was not the only occasion when they were thrown overboard. If a British cruiser gave chase and the dhow was carrying illegal slaves, which most of them were, the captain of the dhow ordered them to be thrown overboard. The ocean-going dhows sailed out of the loading ports at night 'keeping close to the land', Captain Sulivan[8] says, 'with the intention of running their vessels on shore if chased, with the chance of saving some of their

[6] Slave pens.
[7] The crossing of the Atlantic by slavers, from West Africa to the American, was also known as the 'middle passage'.
[8] G. L. Sulivan, *Dhow Chasing in Zanzibar Waters*, 1849-1869.

slaves that are not drowned in the act; and also, if not molested in any way, of touching at the various ports on their way north, to obtain a handful of rice and a cup of water per slave on board, and to fill up the gaps in the cargo caused by the death of many of them....'

Hamed had often seen bloated corpses either washed ashore or still floating in the white surf. Sometimes they would come across a slave clinging to a piece of wood from the wreckage, starved and terrified but still alive, so they pulled him aboard and later sold him in Zanzibar. This was an extra bonus to a small trader like his uncle. It was a game for Hamed and his brother to lean over the sides of the dhow and prod the bodies with their harpoons to discover whether they were dead or alive. Death was an everyday occurrence in their lives, and especially the death of slaves. The beaches in Zanzibar were often strewn with corpses either from the dhows or from the recurring smallpox and cholera epidemics. Like everything else, the epidemics were brought to Zanzibar by the dhows which came with the north-east monsoon. The worse epidemics were in 1858 and 1869 when the island population was decimated and some 50,000 people died. [9]

Dr. Kirk,[10] who spent twenty years on the island and was Agency Surgeon before becoming Consul, despaired of ever preventing the spread of infection. 'It is utterly impossible,' he wrote in a report to the Foreign Office, 'but we must do what we can to remove the accumulation of filth that spreads disease.' This was not easy in normal times when people used the streets and beaches as refuse dumps, but during the epidemics bodies were just thrown on the beaches for the tide to take away. They were mostly slaves and some of them were thrown on the beach before they died in an effort to save the masters from the disease.

By the time the first cholera epidemic struck, Hamed had left the island. When he was about fifteen his father had come to Zanzibar, as he did every few years, to see his bankers and make arrangements for fresh supplies to be sent to Tabora. Also to check that his *banyan*[11] agent was not swindling him on the consignments of ivory and slaves sent to him. On this occasion

[9] In 1858, 20,000 died (at the rate of approximate 250 a day) and in 1869, 30,000 died ("   "   "   "   "   400 " ").
[10] Later Sir John Kirk.
[11] The Hindus were referred to as 'Banyans' by the Zanzibaris.

13

Muhammed at last agreed for his son to join him in Tabora.

Hamed's happiness was complete. He was also prouder than ever of his father because this time Muhammed had come back with his African wife Karunde. Young Hamed was very much impressed by Karunde, not because she was African, but because she was the daughter of the great Chief Fundi Kira, the most powerful chief of Unyamwezi, the large region surrounding Tabora. To be married to a great chief's daughter meant that Muhammed was regarded as a chief himself. Fundi Kira owned enormous stores of ivory, 2,000 head of cattle and unlimited numbers of slaves. 'My father was greatly respected there,' Tippu Tip said. 'Whatever he wanted in and around Tabora he got, and he was given much ivory and other goods by Chief Fundi Kira. My father had many followers and as much property as the chiefs of Uganda,' he boasted to Professor Brode.[12]

Bint Habib bin Bushir, Hamed's mother, was not as enthusiastic as her son about Karunde, but as it was the custom, she accepted the African wife into her house without any fuss. Besides, Karunde may be a chief's daughter, but she, Bint Habib was an Omani Arab, therefore her position was safe.

Muhammed didn't stay long that time. Having arranged with his Indian bankers to advance enough money for the goods he needed, he left with Karunde and a caravan of Wanyamwezi porters. Another caravan would follow a few weeks later with Hamed and his uncle Bushiri. Hamed was disappointed that he couldn't travel with his father, but Muhammed promised he would wait for him in Tabora before going off on a new expedition to Ujiji on Lake Tanganyika.

To keep the Zanzibar market stocked and to repay the money advanced by the bankers, apart from their own profits, the Arab and Swahili traders had to push further and further into the interior of Africa. It was principally to obtain ivory that the traders first penetrated as far as Lake Tanganyika. In the beginning slavery was a side-line to ivory and not as profitable, but as the slaughter of elephants progressed, caravans had to penetrate deeper inland to obtain ivory. This made the transport more expensive and slavery an easier source of revenue and porters.

'The origin of slavery in East Africa is veiled in the glooms of the past,' Richard Burton wrote.[13] 'An institution of the land,

[12] Heinrich Brode, *Tippu Tip*, 1903.
[13] Sir Richard Burton, *The Lake Regions of Central Africa*.

and probably the result of the ancient trade with southern Arabia. At present it is almost universal. With a few exceptions all the tribes, from the eastern equatorial coast to Ujiji and the regions lying westwards of the Tanganyika Lake may be called slave-races. Yet in many parts of the country the tribes are rather slave-importers than exporters. Although they kidnap others, they will not sell their fellows, except when convicted of crime, theft, magic, murder or cutting the upper teeth before the lower. In times of necessity, however, a man will part with his parents, wives, and children, and when they fail he will sell himself without shame. Justice requires the confession that the horrors of slave-driving rarely meet the eye in East Africa ...' he observed.

Burton had been widely criticised for his insensitive approach to the slave-trading problem, and for being critical of the African in general. In comparing the Africans to the Arabs, whom he admired, he used some very unflattering terms and in some regions he considered them almost sub-human. This affected his judgement regarding the 'horrors of slave-driving', although even he recorded cases of unbelievable cruelty. 'There are terrible exceptions,' he wrote, 'as might be expected amongst a people with scant regard for human life. The Kirangozi, or guide, attached to the expedition on return from Ujiji, had loitered behind for some days because his slave girl was too footsore to walk. When tired of waiting he cut off her head, for fear lest she should become gratis another man's property....'

Livingstone didn't find this sort of thing exceptional. He often crossed the slavers' path, and wherever a caravan had passed the evidence of devastation and cruelty enraged him. He describes many instances of men, women and children who had been killed or left tied to a tree for the scavengers to finish off when they couldn't keep up with the caravan, either through illness and exhaustion, or starvation, or both. Mostly they were finished off with a blow from a rifle butt, or their skull smashed with a rock, as in the case of the child whose mother complained that she couldn't go on carrying him *and* the heavy ivory tusk. Ammunition was too precious to waste on a slave. A caravan was normally led by a few Arabs or Waswahili, the rest of the slave drivers, responsible for keeping the caravan moving, were armed slaves and freed slaves. [14] The cruelty of these men was only equalled by the Portuguese half-castes from the coast of Mozam-

[14] The *wangwana* of Zanzibar.

bique, Livingstone noted. 'There is a double purpose in these murders,' he wrote. [15] 'The terror inspired in the minds of the survivors spurs them on to endure the hardships of the march: the Portuguese drovers are quite alive to the merits of this stimulus.'

A caravan could be made up of a few dozen slaves or thousands, depending on the wealth of the trader and his good fortune, but the order of march was very much the same in all caravans. The slaves were roped or chained together in gangs, with their hands tied behind their backs, and if they proved difficult, they had a piece of wood tied into their mouths. If they tried to escape, the man's neck was secured into a cleft stick as thick as a man's thigh, and locked by a cross-bar. Sometimes a double cleft stick was used and one man locked at each end of it. The women were generally roped together by the neck and their children came trailing behind. Some of the women carried infants, and the mortality was incredible. On the march from the interior to the coast, it was calculated that five out of ten slaves died on the way. Livingstone gave an even higher percentage.

To a casual observer this would appear to be mere bad economics on the part of the slavers, but the profit was so enormous, [16] once a slave had been delivered to the Zanzibar market, that the losses never bothered the slaver. The slave had been bought with a few yards of cloth, or even a few handfuls of grain in times of famine. A caravan took four to six months to travel from the lakes to the coast, food was expensive and difficult to obtain en route, and if a slaver lingered along the road to feed and rest the slaves, his profit would have been negligible. Besides, strong healthy slaves were more troublesome and liable to escape.

Another missionary, the Reverend Horace Waller, gave this rather quaint explanation of slave economics: 'It is like sending up for a large block of ice to London in the hot weather. You know that a certain amount will melt away before it reaches you in the country; but that which remains will be quite sufficient for your wants. I have no reason to doubt that four or five lives are lost for every slave sold in Zanzibar.'

The slavers could not always follow the same route. Tribal wars, famine and therefore the inability to obtain provisions, forced them to take longer routes. Later European explorers,

---

[15] David Livingstone's *Last Journals*.
[16] About 60% on every slave.

16

and more often the missionaries, forced caravans to make wide detours to avoid the 'meddling' white man who didn't understand the customs of the land, and therefore interfered. Livingstone, who always went about unarmed, was reckoned to be the biggest nuisance, and many a slaver gave him a wide berth rather than waste time arguing, and often having to release the slaves who were promptly caught and resold by the locals.

However, the route followed by the caravan Hamed was travelling with was the quickest from Bagamoyo [17] to Tabora. Under the supervision of an old and trusted Swahili, Hamed, his uncle and the provisions were loaded on dhows and ferried to Bagamoyo, where the rest of the Wanyamwezi porters were waiting for the return journey to Tabora.

Hamed's training now started in earnest. The five hundred mile journey would take three months if everything went well. Everybody walked. Seven or eight hours a day through dust and heat, mud and rain, wild animals and frightened people, they walked. He had never walked so much in his life. There were no great distances to cover by walking in Zanzibar, and for the first few days his untrained young legs screamed for rest, but he kept walking in front of the caravan, too proud to show his father's porters and slaves that he was weaker than any of them. Even when they camped for the night, he refused to collapse on his sleeping mat. He walked around supervising the slaves as they lit the fires, and the porters as they piled the loads in the middle of the camp. From this first trip he established his reputation. He was never carried, nor would he ride a donkey anywhere. The only time he was carried on a stretcher was at the end of his life as a trader and a slaver.

[17] Bagamoyo means: Lay down the burdens of your heart.

CHAPTER THREE

The First Journey

Tabora was no more than a large mud and wattle village, but the thirty Arabs who lived and traded there had made themselves very comfortable. Their *tembes*[1] were built in the Arab style with inner courtyards, quarters for the women and the house slaves, large shady verandahs, vegetable and fruit gardens, and rice fields.

Muhammed's property at Ituru, a few miles from Tabora, was one of the largest, and hundreds of retainers, slaves and relatives lived there.

The arrival of Hamed's caravan was announced in the traditional manner with volley after volley of gunfire, and everybody rushed out to meet them. The welcome was not just for Hamed. The safe arrival of a caravan was always an event and a reason for celebration, but Hamed was wide-eyed with wonder as the feasting went on through the night.

As they sat on cushions and carpets on the large verandah, more and more people came up to meet the son of Muhammed and more and more platters of rice, chicken and mutton were brought out from the kitchens where Muhammed's women worked under Karunde's supervision. The little coffee cups were continually refilled by a slave carrying a huge *birika*[2] and bowls of sweetmeats were placed by each guest. Out on the yard the porters entertained their friends and relatives with tales of life at the coast. There was a lot of shouting and laughing as they roasted the ox Muhammed had given them, and drank the

[1] Unlike the Africans' round mud huts, a tembe was square or oblong and mostly built of mud and stone. Only Arabs and chiefs built this type of house.
[2] Arab brass coffee pot.

18

pombe [3] the women had brewed. Later there was singing and dancing in the compound by the porters' huts and as the drums went on beating, Hamed's eyes were closing with exhaustion, but he was determined to stay awake as long as his father and his guests.

'Time for you to sleep, my son,' Muhammed finally said as the last guest left. 'Karunde has sent a very nice girl to your bed. There's nothing better than the soft flesh of a woman for a tired man.'

Hamed had been given a comfortable room and he didn't want a woman tonight. All he wanted was sleep on a soft bed. He hadn't seen a bed for three months, but he smiled at his father. 'Thank you, baba. Have you decided when we go on a trading trip together?' he added.

'Plenty of time to speak about that. I'm waiting for news from Ugangi. There's fighting there now and when it's over, there'll be plenty for us to trade.' [4]

Muhammed was referring to the seasonal tribal fighting which kept the local markets well stocked with slaves. 'All African wars,' Burton wrote, [5] 'are for one of two objects, cattle lifting and kidnapping. Some of the pastoral tribes assert the theory that none but themselves have a right to possess herds, and they received the gift directly from their ancestor who created cattle; in practice they covet the animals for the purpose of a general gorge. Slaves, however, are much more frequently the end and aim of feud and foray. The process of kidnapping, an inveterate custom in these lands, is in every way agreeable to the mind of the man-hunter. A poor and powerful chief will not allow his neighbours to rest wealthier than himself; a quarrel is soon found, the stronger attacks the weaker, hunts and harries his cattle, burns his villages, carries off his subjects and sells them to the first passing caravan ...'

In all the explorers' writings, even in Stanley's, although he was always in a hurry to get from one point to another, one reads of whole regions being 'devastated'. Villages and crops burnt to the ground, the few remaining people hiding in fear, and always skeletons, skeletons everywhere.

It has been suggested by a number of modern writers that the

[3] African beer also known as tembo.
[4] Murjebi Family Papers.
[5] Richard Burton's *The Lake Regions of Central Africa*, 1860.

19

evil of slavery would have never plagued Africa had the foreign slavers not brought it with them. This seems unlikely when one examines the history of the world in general. The capture of slaves has always been the reward of the winner, and Africa was no exception. It is true that the advent of the Arab slave-trader in East Africa increased and encouraged the trade, but the practice had always existed. The Arabs provided an ever-hungry market for slaves, they promoted and supported wars between chiefs, and by the power of their guns, they controlled huge areas, as in the case of Tippu Tip, who controlled and exploited an area half the size of Europe.

'Bribes were offered to us three times by Manyema chiefs to assist them in destroying their neighbours, to whom they are of near kin, and with whom they have almost daily intimate relations,' Stanley wrote. [6] 'Our refusal of ivory and slaves appeared to surprise the chiefs, and they expressed the opinion that we white men were not as good as the Arabs, for—though it was true we did not rob them of their wives, ravish and steal their daughters, enslave their sons, or despoil them of a single article—the Arabs would have assisted them. One of my men, who knew Manyema of old, said, "I told you, master, what kind of people these were: they have always got a little war on hand, and they wait the arrival of the Arabs to begin." They are humble and liberal to the strong-armed Arab, savage and murderous and cannibalistic to small bands, and every slain man provides a banquet of meat for the forest natives of Manyema.'

War and raids were not the only means by which a chief provided himself with slaves. With the help of his trusted witch-doctor, he could thin out his own population in times of need. Since the whole family of a criminal was sold into slavery as a matter of course, 'it affords a scope for the tyranny of a chief,' Burton wrote, [7] 'who, if powerful enough, will enrich himself by vending his subjects in wholesale and retail. By weakening the tie of family, it acts with deadly effect in preventing the increase of the race.'

Sir Reginald Coupland [8] estimated that in the 1870s the annual loss of Africans to East Africa, by enslavement and slaughter, was from 80,000 to 100,000. One explorer suggested that anti-slavery

[6] H. M. Stanley's *Through the Dark Continent*, 1874-1877.
[7] Richard Burton's *The Lake Regions of Central Africa*, 1860.
[8] Reginald Coupland's *East Africa and Its Invaders*, 1938.

20

measures were unnecessary as the near future would see the complete depopulation of the country.

One may ask why the majority of slaves never escaped or rebelled. The country was vast and the slavers were a tiny minority compared to the captured. Traders like Tippu Tip had an enormous following of slaves. He was always accompanied by a group of 'young Arabs', as Stanley describes them, and a well armed escort of freed-slaves, but the majority of his followers *were* slaves. The fear of punishment if caught and the fear of the gun, were two strong deterrents to escape, although most of Tippu Tip's slaves were armed and fought side by side with the Arabs and the 'freedmen'. If one escaped from an Arab slaver one was almost certain to be recaptured by the local tribe, either to be sold to a chief, or back to the original owner, or worse as 'cannibal fodder', as when Tippu Tip operated in the Upper Congo regions.

During one of his expeditions in Tetera country, his uncle Bushiri, 10 Zanzibaris and 50 Wanyamwezi porters were eaten by the local cannibals. This was the signal for another punitive campaign, and the most powerful of the local chiefs, Kasongo, insisted on taking part in the expedition. Tippu Tip says that a force of 100,000 men was involved. As usual they marched from place to place killing and burning, and most of the male prisoners were eaten by Chief Kasongo's followers. 'Two of them eating a whole man,' Tippu Tip said. [9] He tried to put a stop to the carnage, less out of love for his neighbour than because the sickening smell of the slaughtered human flesh upset him. The cannibals however ignored him. 'If we are not to eat of men's flesh, do you refrain from goat's flesh?' they asked him. 'In the face of this reasonable argument, things remained as they were,' he says. After two months, Tippu Tip agreed that justice had been well served, and the local population left alive paid an indemnity of sixty elephant tusks and the victor's army withdrew.

From this incident it may seem that Tippu Tip was a heartless man. In fact he was less cruel than most of the Arab slavers and the local chiefs. Even Livingstone admitted that much.

Through most of his career as a trader in 'white and black ivory', as the Victorians quaintly referred to ivory and slaves, Tippu Tip enjoyed the friendship and trust of the Sultans of Zanzibar. As he provided these rulers with a large part of their

[9] *Maisha ya Hamed bin Mohammed el Murjebi, yaani Tippu Tip.*

revenue, the Sultans' regard for Tippu Tip was not unnatural.

Tippu Tip was of course a loyal supporter of the Sultans, but on the mainland he was a law unto himself and took orders from no-one. At the head of his caravans, like all Arab caravans, a slave carried the Sultan's red flag, but that was the extent of the Sultan's influence on Tippu Tip the man, or his dominions.

The red flag preceded Muhammed's caravan, when he took his young son on his first trading expedition to Ugangi, north-east of Lake Nyasa. The goods to be traded for were as usual, elephant tusks and slaves. It was not a very large caravan, but it served well for Tippu Tip's initial training.

First and most important, the *pagazi*, or African porters, had to be found, and in this respect his father had no difficulty in obtaining all he wanted from his father-in-law in Tabora. As it happens, the Wanyamwezi were well known as the best porters in East Africa. Even Stanley, the most demanding of masters, found them superior to other tribes. 'While explorers would prefer the Wangwana (freed slaves) as escort, the Wanyamwezi are far superior as porters,' he wrote,[10] 'their greater freedom from disease, their great strength and endurance, the pride they take in their profession of porters, prove them born travellers of incalculable use and benefit to Africa. Their courage they have repeatedly proved under their Napoleonic leader Mirambo, in many a well-fought field against the Arab and Wangwana. Tippu-Tip has led 500 of these men through distant Bisa and the plains of Rua ... The English discoverer of Lake Tanganyika,[11] and, finally, I myself have been equally indebted to them, both on my first and last expeditions. From their numbers, and their many excellent qualities, I am led to think that the day will come when they will be regarded as something better than the "best pagazis"; that they will be esteemed as the good subjects of some enlightened power, who will train them up as the nucleus of a great African nation, as powerful for the good of the Dark Continent, as they threaten, under the present condition of things, to be for its evil....' All this some seventy-five years before the birth of the independent nation of Tanzania.

Tippu Tip's father, was therefore, lucky to have the Wanyamwezi as porters.

[10] H. M. Stanley's *In Darkest Africa*, 1887-1889.
[11] Stanley was not a great admirer of Richard Burton, the discoverer of Lake Tanganyika.

The next most important thing to prepare for such an expedition, were the loads, and they had to be given the greatest care. Each porter carried a 60 lbs. load and these included goods to be used for barter at their destination, goods to be traded on the road for the food the caravan consumed, and other loads were prepared for *hongo*. [12] A very important element in any caravan, whether Arab or European, trading or exploring. The hongo paid, very much depended on the strength of the chief and the strength of the caravan. It varied from a few yards of *merikani*, [13] to whole bales. Apart from various types of cloth, [14] the traders and the explorers carried cowry shells, [15] coloured beads and coils of copper and wire. The goods taken on an expedition, varied according to the likes and dislikes of the people in the different regions, but cotton, beads and wire, were universally accepted. The explorers were plagued by the exorbitant demands for hongo, and in most cases they paid dearly for their inexperience and unwillingness to use force. The Arabs were not often faced with these problems if they travelled with an armed escort. If a chief and his subjects became unreasonable, an Arab trading expedition became a punitive expedition and the situation was speedily resolved, unless the over-demanding chief happened to be Mirambo. Of Mirambo we will speak later, at the time of Tippu Tip's first trip, the future 'Napoleonic leader', was still a child looking after his father's goats.

The quantity and quality of loads, and consequently of porters, varied greatly from one explorer to the other. Livingstone carried the bare minimum and most of it was stolen from him, just before he met Tippu Tip. By then he was desperately ill and the loss of his medicine chest brought his death a little closer. Stanley, at the other end of the scale, carried everything he could possibly need under any condition. Portable bath-tubs and Fortnum & Mason's hampers stocked with paté-de-foie-gras and other essentials, were prominent features of his luggage. The explorers depended very much on the advice they received in Zanzibar before embarking on their African journeys. The consuls and the Indian merchants advised in rather different ways,

[12] The fee which every caravan had to pay various chiefs in order to be allowed to march through their country.
[13] White cotton cloth which originally came from America.
[14] White of coloured cotton was more acceptable than silk.
[15] Cowry shells were the only legal tender acceptable in some parts.

23

but Stanley knew what he wanted. When he went in search of Livingstone and finally found him at Ujiji, not only was Livingstone surprised to see a white face and being greeted with the famous, 'Doctor Livingstone, I presume'; but the greatest surprise was in store for the poor starving missionary when Stanley produced a 'bottle of choice champagne' to celebrate their meeting. This doesn't mean that Stanley always travelled with champagne in his luggage, it just shows that even on his first African journey, he knew what he might need, and he would need champagne if he met the only other white man in Central Africa.

Tippu Tip was always fascinated by Stanley's mode of travelling. Boats for the crossing of lakes and rivers, special tents, special boots and most of all—special guns. Repeating guns, which made Tippu Tip's eyes blink faster than any store of ivory. Guns were power to Tippu Tip, and the kind of power Stanley held in his hands, the slaver had never seen before. Ammunition too played a very important part in the success of any expedition, whether punitive or peaceful, and Stanley never seemed to run out of that.

Tippu Tip's first trip with his father was a peaceful one. They reached Ugangi, some three hundred miles from Tabora, in very good time. They walked six or seven hours a day, with rests in between and covered the distance in less than two months. Their trading in Ugangi having gone according to schedule, his father decided they should head back for the coast and sell their acquisitions in Zanzibar before going back to Tabora. An all round trip of approximately one thousand miles on foot. Very few Arabs rode donkeys as some of the areas they crossed were infested with tsetse flies. Stanley made ample use of 'pack donkeys' and 'riding asses' but these didn't go very far inland before they got sick and died. [16]

Tippu Tip was always very proud of his ability to out-walk anybody and never giving in to fatigue or illness. He was very strong and healthy and despite the occasional attack of malaria, he had enormous powers of recovery and endurance. In later life, when he was a good deal older and richer, he liked to tell people that he walked to show that in the eyes of God he remained the humble trader he had always been.

However, travelling back from Zanzibar to Tabora, after their

[16] He even brought dogs. Bull-terriers he says, but from the picture of the last one to die, Jock, they look exactly like boxers.

expedition to Ugangi, Tippu Tip was stricken with small-pox, but maybe because of his youth and already determined character, after a few days of resting by the roadside, he insisted they should continue on their march. They had no medicines and any disease was left to take its course. You either survived and went on with the caravan, or you perished and the hyenas and jackals took care of you.

When small-pox struck a caravan, it went through it like wild fire as nobody was quarantined in the middle of Africa. The only quarantine they knew, in the case of slaves or even porters, was to leave them behind when they became sick. If they survived they were told to catch up at the next camp. Sometimes the sick man built himself a shelter of twigs and branches, and if he was lucky he was left his ration of food and water, but no caravan would await the sick. It was different when sickness affected dozens of porters and the loads couldn't be redistributed amongst the others, then the whole caravan had to stop. Dysentery and malaria were not uncommon among Arabs and Africans, but they were not considered fatal or even important, whereas in the case of Europeans, most of the deaths were caused by these two diseases. Despite their medicine boxes, their hygiene, mosquito nets and sun helmets, a large percentage of Europeans who came to Africa in those days died of dysentery or malaria, or both.

Tippu Tip had contracted small-pox in Zanzibar but he was lucky because not only did he recover but he was not disfigured. 'The disease left no pock-marks on Tippu Tip who was no beauty anyway,' Brode wrote. [17] Some people considered him handsome. Stanley did and the women certainly did, but the pictures rather support Brode's opinion. Nevertheless, he had a good figure, and his elegance of bearing and dress made him a striking man.

Tippu Tip and his father had also been lucky in other respects on that trip. Slaves were selling better than ever in Zanzibar. According to Captain Devereux, [18] forty thousand slaves were bought and sold on the East African coast and in Zanzibar in 1859. 'We are rather struck with the increase of dhow trade,' he wrote. 'Almost hourly these primitive vessels arrive with crowded cargoes of slaves, crossing our bows with the greatest impunity. We once more visit the Slave Market and there find

[17] Heinrich Brode, *Tippu Tip*, 1903.
[18] Capt. W. C. Devereux, *A Cruise in the Gordon*, 1869.

25

fresh vigour; the traffic seems to have gained new life since our last visit. The market is full: fierce Arabs, Turks and Abyssinians are busy with their bargains. Negroes are trotted out in a business-like way; women are felt and squeezed. Their legs, ankles and teeth are examined most disgustingly and unfeelingly by the dealers. They are far dearer than ever, and more bought and sold. The purchasers are continually walking off with files of blacks, no doubt taken to the general depot, whence they will be carried northward in the dreadful dhows....'

The strong old Sultan, Seyyid Said, had died two years (1856) before Devereux's visit to Zanzibar[19] and Seyyid Majid who succeeded him was young, inexperienced and irresolute. A new British Consul, Colonel Rigby,[20] was his only help in controlling a rebellion instigated by his brother Barghash and supported by the French. With all his troubles the new Sultan could do very little to curb the ever increasing slave trade.

Some of the 'fashions' had changed, but essentially the trade continued despite the British naval and diplomatic efforts. The slaves were painted in colourful stripes in Captain Smee's time; they wore red caps in Burton's time, and eye make-up in Devereux's time, but basically there were no changes in the method of sale.

The location of the market was different since Tippu Tip had left Zanzibar. Seyyid Said had moved it from Changani to Kirungani 'by way of a sop to the British Cerberus', Burton says, but this site was eventually found inconvenient and the market was moved again to a place which is now almost the centre of Zanzibar town, and where the Cathedral of Christ Church was built by the Universities Mission to Central Africa in 1877. The altar stands where the whipping post once stood. The whipping post itself was made into a cross, and the Sultan (by then Barghash) presented a clock for the tower.

This great change in the Zanzibaris' way of life was not to be for some years. Meanwhile Tippu Tip and his father were well satisfied with the state of the market. The hardships of a thousand miles' walk had all been very worth-while.

[19] Devereux arrived in Zanzibar in 1858.
[20] *General Rigby, Zanzibar & the Slave Trade*, written by his daughter, Mrs. Russell, in 1935.

CHAPTER FOUR

An Independent Trader

When towards the end of his life Tippu Tip told his story to Professor Brode, he showed an amazing power of recollection for places, battles and the names of the chiefs involved. He remembered every skirmish, the exact number of elephant tusks, as well as the price and the weight of the ivory he bought and sold throughout his career; but he was not greatly interested in dates. He talks of the time of the cholera, and the time of the famine; or the time of this and that Sultan's death. The other thing he was not much interested in discussing with a white infidel, was his love life. So it isn't surprising that his Arab wife is only mentioned once in Brode's book and only to point out how Tippu Tip had been able to buy fifty thousand dollars' worth of goods. 'At this time I had no shamba or house in Zanzibar, nor any property at all, but I did have a wife, Bint Salum bin Abdulla el Barwanije. She had many riches here in Zanzibar and Muscat.' [1]

In fact, Bint Salum had been Tippu Tip's wife for quite a number of years before the restocking for the next expedition. The arrangements had been made between the two families before Tippu Tip joined his father in Tabora and the wedding took place during his first visit to Zanzibar. It was an important event in his life as the fifteen year old bride came from 'a rich and respected Muscat family', Tippu Tip said. Like his father before him, it was important that he should have a pure Arab as a legal first wife. Bint Salum was the mother of his eldest son, Sef, who would eventually take over the family business as Tippu Tip was now taking over from his father. Of course, he had a

[1] Heinrich Brode's *Tippu Tip*.

27

great number of concubines. Nobody would expect differently from a man, and an Arab at that, who was away from home for over thirty years. He took other wives, and more than he could cope with were offered to him by the various chiefs he did business with. From them he had many children, but none as important as Sef.

Part of the harem followed him on the many expeditions, others were left behind at his headquarters and depots in the various centres. He was a demanding master but kinder and more generous than most Arab traders. His women were always dressed in the finest clothes and bangles, and he never forgot to bring them presents when he returned from his trips. The women adored him. It was nothing, as Livingstone reported, for a young woman from Tippu Tip's harem to run ahead of the caravan. She would 'run at a sharp trot', decked out in her finery and followed by her personal slaves carrying supplies, pots and pans, and all that was needed to make sure that when her master arrived at a new camp he would find his favourite food, a bath, clean robes and a ready couch. All who knew Tippu Tip, remarked on his elegant appearance, and his women made sure that all was ready for him when he clapped his hands.

The strict rules of the harem were somewhat relaxed when he marched from one region to another, but where he settled down for any length of time, the harem became once more a closely guarded house. Such establishments were under the supervision of one of his Mohammedan wives, and if not pure Arabs, they were at least Swahilis from the coast or one of the other settlements. These women ran the harem like headmistresses of a girls' boarding school, and their power was only inferior to that of the master himself.

When one of these Mohammedan wives died Tippu Tip was much upset. All the honours that were not accorded to her during her life, were granted in death. Whilst the other women wailed and cried in the courtyard, her body was brought out onto the verandah where she had never been allowed to sit in her lifetime, strapped to the underside of her bed to signify that she had left her rightful place in this world, and all the Arabs of the settlement passed by the bed and paid their last respects by kissing the draperies. Last came Tippu Tip, his head bowed in sorrow. As he approached the bed his relatives bowed low with their hands crossed over their breasts. He removed his sandals and placed them on her bed. They were the sandals he wore when he went to her private room, and by having them buried with her, he was conveying to the other women that they could never take her place.

Many years after his own death, the wife of one of his sons was asked to speak about her famous father-in-law, and she said: 'He was the kindest man who ever lived. His slaves regarded him as their father.' She had been married to his son when she was thirteen and spoke of her father-in-law as the greatest man she had ever known. According to her, Tippu Tip's household in Zanzibar was always ready waiting for him. 'My husband was all right,' the old lady said. 'He was just a rich man's son. I got his house in order and when I became old, knowing what men are like, I picked out his concubines for him. I picked out good serious girls, but my husband was never the man his father was. Everyone worshipped his father.'

Being a devout Mohammedan he never drank or smoked and although he had dozens of concubines, his 'brains were never softened by the sexual excesses of the harem', one white missionary remarked. He rarely spent a night without a woman on his sleeping mat or couch, but the endless search for ivory and slaves was his first love and from the very beginning nothing else really mattered to Tippu Tip.

When he returned to Tabora after the first trip with his father, he needed to recover from the attack of small-pox, and for two months he was taken care of by Karunde and her slaves. He had already acquired a number of his own, both male and female, so life in Ituru, his father's property near Tabora, was very pleasant, but not pleasant enough to keep Tippu Tip away from trading. At the end of the two months he was on his way to Ujiji, on Lake Tanganyika, with his father 'and others of his kin', to trade for ivory and 'other goods'. He always spoke of 'other goods' to his biographer but rarely mentioned slaves. In fact, reading Tippu Tip's narrative one becomes convinced that the old rogue was nothing more than a good trader of ivory who was often forced to defend himself from the unsolicited attacks of the local chiefs, and incidentally had to take a few prisoners. After all, by the time Brode recorded Tippu Tip's memoirs in 1903, slavery was supposed to be a thing of the past.

At the end of the 1850s no such problems bothered the young Tippu Tip. The real problem was the Ujiji market which had very little to offer the Tabora traders at that time. They found that ivory and slaves were too expensive and of inferior quality, and they decided to cross the lake and go on to Urua, a region west of the lake on the fringe of the Arab trading frontiers and as yet almost unknown.

Tippu Tip's father, however, decided to go back to Tabora. His fortune was made and he was no longer interested in extending his territory. The comforts of home were now more important to old Muhammed. He entrusted his son and the precious barter goods to an old hand, a Swahili from the coast, and prepared for the return journey. Young Tippu Tip was most indignant about the arrangement.

'I can't go along to Urua with all our goods entrusted to a man from the coast,' he said to his father. 'Why should I take orders from a Swahili. If you don't trust me more than you trust him, I had better go back to Tabora with you.'

Muhammed was a little surprised but obviously pleased at his son's indignation. 'I wouldn't have given the stuff to the man if you had been older and more experienced,' he said. 'But if you think you can look after the goods yourself, so much the better.'

'Well, try it this time,' Tippu Tip said. 'If I fail, you can send somebody else next time.' [2]

He took charge of their goods without further argument, determined to prove to his father that he was as good a trader as any Arab in the caravan, and certainly better than any Swahili half-caste. Even then he would have killed any man who suggested that he was a half-caste himself.

With twenty Arabs and their retinue of slaves, porters and guards, he crossed the lake in great dug-out canoes. The only type of vessel used on Lake Tanganyika at that time.

As soon as they reached the village of a friendly chief, Mrongo Tambwe, he set about establishing his reputation as one of the most cunning Arab traders the region had ever known. Whereas the other Arabs bought the large expensive tusks, Tippu Tip bought the smallest and cheapest. [3] There was good reasoning behind his choice. During his last visit to Zanzibar he had noticed

[2] Murjebi Family Papers.

[3] The large tusks (were) known as *Babu Ulaya* because they were used in Europe (Ulaya) to make billiard balls and piano keys, and the smaller ones were known as *Babu Katchi* (Kutch) because they were exported to India to make bangles and ornaments.

30

a glut of large tusks on the market and he decided to take a gamble on the smaller ones. By the time he got back to Zanzibar there was a great shortage of Babu Katchi and he made an enormous profit, selling them at about 55 dollars per *frasila*, [4] a record price for the normally inferior tusks.

However, it took Tippu Tip quite a number of months to get back to Zanzibar with his precious load of ivory. On the way back to Lake Tanganyika he learnt that Chief Fundi Kira of Tabora had died and that Manwa Sera, a nephew of the old chief, had been chosen as the new chief with Muhammed's support. This was not a popular move. Another relation of the old chief, Mkasiwa, immediately fortified his village and declared war. The newly elected chief, Manwa Sera, in turn attacked the rebels but without much success. The fighting dragged on for weeks until Manwa Sera decided he needed the support of the Tabora Arabs to defeat his enemy, and the only way to get the Arabs' help, was through Muhammed bin Juma. A large stock of ivory changed hands and the Arabs joined the fight. The rebels were either killed or captured, but Mkasiwa escaped. Unfortunately for the Arabs, the victory went to Manwa Sera's head and he soon forgot his debt. He was the great victor and he could make any rule he liked, one of them being that all Arab caravans going through his territory must pay him hongo. The Arabs were furious but helpless. Their leader and the most powerful Arab in the region, Muhammed bin Juma, was still supporting Manwa Sera. After all, he was related to the chief by marriage to Karunde.

It was unfortunate for Chief Manwa Sera that drink [5] and power do not mix. In one of his more drunken moments he executed Karunde's mother and brother, a gesture which was not appreciated by Karunde's husband, Muhammed. Unlike a European son-in-law, Muhammed very much objected to his mother-in-law being disposed of in such a manner. Muhammed was furious and his son Tippu Tip arrived back in Tabora just in time to lend his support to the old man. It was decided that Manwa Sera should be taught a lesson. 'This fellow, Manwa Sera has done away with my in-laws, and I intend to fight him,' [6]

[4] One *frasila* was 35 lbs. and the Austrian Maria Theresa dollar, which was still in use then, was about 4 dollars to the pound sterling. Much later the currency was changed to Indian *Pice*.

[5] He was known as the *Tembo Drinker*.

[6] Murjebi Family Papers.

old Muhammed said to his son, and fight they did. The rebel Mkasiwa was brought back, all was made ready, 'a great feast was eaten', and the 400 Arabs with their slaves and followers attacked. The number of Arabs in Tabora at that time was greater than usual as quite a lot of them had escaped from Zanzibar following the unsuccessful revolt against Sultan Majid.

Before his death in 1856, Seyyid Said had made a will by which his third son, Majid was to inherit the small islands of Zanzibar,[7] Pemba, Mafia and the coastal strip; and another son would inherit the throne of Oman.

Majid was not Said's favourite son, but his first choice had died and so Majid, the son of a secondary Circassian wife, frail, moody, shifty and an epileptic, ascended the throne and unleashed all the old troubles that his father had so successfully settled.

The brother in Oman, dissatisfied with his share of the old Sultan's heritage, threatened to invade Zanzibar. The French on the island of Reunion renewed their efforts to secure a dominant influence in Zanzibar and a foothold on the mainland, and at home in Zanzibar, the rich and powerful el-Harthy tribe began to make trouble for Majid. They secured the help of his younger brother Barghash, a much stronger character and more than ready to dispossess his weak brother.

When he first ascended the throne, Majid had his father's friend and adviser, British Consul Hamerton to help him; but when he too suddenly died and no substitute was sent for a year, the situation deteriorated rapidly.

This was the boiling pot in which the new British Consul Rigby landed in 1858. Looting, killing and firing of clove plantations had been going on for sometime, but a few months after Rigby's arrival the younger brother Barghash and his supporters entrenched themselves at Machui, four miles from the town and known as 'Marseilles', and the rebellion started in earnest. Majid formally requested the assistance of the British navy from Rigby, and one hundred marines, twelve officers and a 12-pound gun went to support the legal sovereign. Within a few days a tearful Barghash handed his sword over to Rigby.

Barghash was exiled to Bombay and most of the rebels escaped to the mainland. Those who went to Tabora were involved in the fight against Manwa Sera. It took the Arabs over three months to defeat the *tembo drinker*, and both sides lost 'com-

[7] 54 miles long by 24 miles wide.

parable numbers', according to Tippu Tip's cool evaluation. But the expenses of the war would be compensated for by the sale of the captured enemy, and finally Tippu Tip collected his share of the booty and started for the coast followed by a large caravan carrying his own small tusks and his father's large stock.

Allah was very good to him. The small tusks and the slaves had sold well and he was ready to enjoy life. So he sold his father's ivory and with the profit bought the supplies old Muhammed had ordered and sent them back to Tabora. Tippu Tip then decided to spend a few years trading on the mainland as far as Urori, about 200 miles inland, and passed a little time with his young wife and son. He quickly made a reputation for himself on the Zanzibar market as a capable and reliable trader, and so he had no trouble in obtaining barter goods on credit from the *banyans*. Within a very short time he doubled his business and made tremendous profits.

At this time he met his half brother again, Muhammed bin Masud, the son of another legal wife of old Muhammed, whom he had not seen for ten years. They had traded together on the coast when they were small boys, but then Tippu Tip had joined his father and Muhammed, after some trading inland, had gone to sea in the family dhows, and the two boys had not met again.

Tippu Tip was so pleased to be reunited with his brother that he decided to go into partnership with him, and together strike out a new route to the southern end of Lake Tanganyika.

'There are great profits to be made, brother,' he said. 'Few people know the place and we will make great fortunes.' [8]

His brother was enthusiastic. He borrowed just over a thousand pounds in goods, but Tippu Tip managed to borrow *eight* thousand pounds from 'some twenty Indians and Banyans' for this expedition. For a young trader still in his early twenties, this was quite an achievement, and it says a lot for his business skill and reputation.

The Indians often lost all their investments, either through the caravan being decimated by African attacks, or the leaders being killed and their followers escaping with all the goods, or the leader himself absconding with all the supplies. If the debtor came back, the profits were very great of course, and as the

[8] Murjebi Family Papers.

Indians were the 'cash box' for all Arab expeditions, and most Arabs disliked the keeping of accounts, few money lenders showed a loss. *Wanabahatisha sana*, they have a lot of luck, the Swahili used to say about the Indians.

CHAPTER FIVE

Chief Samu and Dr. Livingstone

Tippu Tip left nothing to luck. He took risks but always calculated risks, and to this, his greatest venture to date, he gave all his care and attention.

Eight thousand pounds' worth of goods were collected, transported by dhow to Bagamoyo on the mainland, divided into loads, and 700 Wanyamwezi porters engaged for the long march to Lake Tanganyika. They had not gone very far inland when the porters realised that their employer had no intention of following the usual route back to Tabora through Usagara and Ugogo, but instead was heading south towards Urori.

Before leaving Bagamoyo, Tippu Tip had paid the porters [1] half their wages, but the rations [2] were distributed to them every few days. They only ate once a day when they made camp for the night, and it was always a gourd full of crushed millet or maize cooked like a thick porridge with a few beans or other vegetables added to it. [3]

Before entering Urori, Tippu Tip distributed rations for the following six days and ordered the caravan to stop and rest for two days. As usual during a long stop-over, the porters scattered through the surrounding villages in search of food, hospitality and women, and only returned to camp when the 'departure drums were sounded'. This invasion by foreign porters was not always

[1] Porters were always paid in kind. Usually with lengths of cloth. Half their wages they received before leaving, and the other half was paid to them on arrival to discourage deserters.

[2] Each porter was given rice or millet or posho (ground maize), depending on availability and regions. For the rest they had to fend for themselves.

[3] Meat was only eaten on very special occasions and never by women and children.

35

welcome to the locals, because there was often looting, raping and killing, but unless it endangered the progress of the caravan, Tippu Tip never interfered with his followers. In his opinion every man had a right to food and women, and if they managed to catch one or two slaves, this all added to their buying power at the next market.

On the third day Tippu Tip ordered the drums to be sounded, but no porter appeared. He sent men of his armed escort to search the villages, but no porters could be found anywhere. All the 700 had deserted with their six days' supply of food and wages. Any other trader at that point would have despaired and returned to the coast, but no other trader's name has left a mark on the history of East Africa.

'I lost my temper,' Tippu Tip says. He was not one to waste words, but he immediately took action. He left his brother in charge of the camp and the loads, and with his bed-roll and a small force of armed followers, he retraced his steps and forced the surrounding villages to give him porters. The Wazaramu had never worked as porters, and the news that a force of armed Arabs was on the war path quickly spread around the country. Every village he entered was deserted of man-power.

This small obstacle was overcome quite easily. He had 200 village elders and their families tied together and a few shots fired. Not too many. Ammunition was precious. An agreement was immediately reached and the village drums frantically re-called the men hiding in the bush. No further objections were raised and the new porters were driven off by Tippu Tip's men. 'I went into every part of Zaramu country,' he says,[4] 'and within five days had seized eight-hundred men. They called me *Kingugwa*, the leopard, because the leopard catches here and there. I yoked the whole lot of them together and went back with them to Nkamba.'

Having brought the new recruits into camp, he was not taking any more chances with deserters. He went off to a village where a *banyan* had a trading duka,[5] bought all the metal he could find and marched back to camp where he ordered his own blacksmith to make chains. 'I put all the porters in chains and made my brother walk ahead of them,' he said. 'I followed behind, so that I could catch anyone who tried to escape. Those *washenzi*

[4] *Maisha ya Hamed bin Muhammed el Murjebi, yaani Tippu Tip.*
[5] Shop.

called my brother Kumbakumba, which means, he who takes everyone,' he added indignantly. [4]

Now that he had solved his porters' problem, he only allowed short stops to barter for food and to assess the country's potentials. He left one of his Swahili followers to trade in Urori and his brother with a small force and fifteen guns to trade with another minor chief, but he pushed on, covering hundreds of miles with the eight-hundred porters, his Arab and Swahili followers, some of whom were relatives, and one hundred armed guards, towards Lake Tanganyika and beyond to Itawa and the legendary Chief Samu; the wealthiest and most powerful chief of all.

They all tried to dissuade him. Even the porters, now no longer in chains because they were too far from their country to think of escape, appealed to him. After all he was the only man who could safely lead them back to their villages, and they were terrified by the stories they had heard of Samu's power and cruelty. 'You will not return,' the guides warned him. 'You are only bringing him goods. He's got plenty of ivory but he'll never give you any. He is treacherous,' they said. [6] Tippu Tip took no notice and marched on. They met an old Arab trader who was giving Samu's country a wide berth, and he told them how Samu had once taken all his goods and killed most of his men. 'However, we did not take his advice but went on,' [6] Tippu Tip says with unmistakable determination. He crossed the river Lofu and marched into Itawa, Samu's kingdom.

By then, his brother Muhammed had caught up with him, and they all realised that this was the richest country they had ever seen. Plantation followed plantation, and thousands of people tended the crops. 'The villages were numerous and large, and *at that time* [7] the area was densely populated,' he says. [6] There was an air of prosperity about the place which pleased Tippu Tip enormously, and although the people were most unfriendly to the new intruders, nobody tried to stop them. Only the villages where a chief was in residence were fortified, and these chiefs were relations of the great Samu, but even they did nothing to stop the advancing caravan.

After marching for six days and passing hundreds of villages, they finally came to a hill and clustered at the foot of it, Samu's

---

[6] *Maisha ya Hamed bin Muhammed el Murjebi, yaani Tippu Tip.*
[7] My italics.

village. It was the largest they had seen and strongly fortified. Three rows of stockades, ditches and thorn bushes surrounded it and the gates were firmly locked.

Tippu Tip ordered the caravan to stop some distance from the stockade and sent a young Arab and a guide carrying the red flag of Zanzibar who spoke the local language, with gifts and messages of peace for Chief Samu. The messengers never reached the gates. A shower of arrows hit and wounded them, but Tippu Tip decided there was no point in starting a fight then. His men needed rest and food, he needed more information about Samu's forces, and besides there was plenty of time to teach Chief Samu that he was not dealing with any ordinary trader.

They camped and posted sentries and the next morning Chief Samu must have had a change of heart because he sent a message ordering them to bring presents. The messenger was escorted by a large party of arrogant warriors who held their spears at the ready and surrounded the camp. Once again Tippu Tip restrained himself. As ordered he went to the village with his uncle and three other Arabs, but all unarmed and followed by slaves carrying the gifts of cloth and beads. Much more than he usually gave other chiefs, but he wanted to be sure of a good reception. He much preferred to trade without fighting.

They were led to a huge round hut where the old chief was reclining on a pile of skins, surrounded by elders, warriors and women. Chief Samu was an enormously fat man and almost ninety years old. He was so fat that he never walked. He had to be carried everywhere. He ordered his slaves to show him the gifts the Arabs had brought and his small yellow eyes greedily darted from the cloth to the beads and back again. He never acknowledged the Arabs nor spoke to them, but he signalled and his slaves lifted him onto a stretcher also covered with skins. Everybody followed the stretcher to a store twice the size of Samu's quarters and the doors were flung open to reveal piles and piles of ivory tusks. For the first time the old chief looked directly at Tippu Tip who was blinking uncontrollably at the sight of all that ivory, and smiling a malevolent and toothless grin he clapped his hands once and the doors were shut again.

Tippu Tip was stunned. It was customary for a chief who had received presents to give a few tusks as a sign of friendship to his guests. But not Samu. He offered nothing, he just clapped his hands and the whole cortege headed back for his *tembe*.

Trying to control his temper, Tippu Tip caught up with the stretcher and smiling at the reclining chief, he said: 'Sultan, you are so rich and powerful, can't you even spare a tusk for an honest trader?'

The chief was furious and shaking with anger he shouted for his guards to throw the Arabs out of the village. The excited crowds followed and pushed them towards the gates and it was difficult for the Arabs to walk away with dignity. However they followed their leader quietly and finally reached their camp. 'Well, that was a waste of good cloth and beads,' Tippu Tip said. 'We'll have to think of another way to make the old *shenzi* give up his ivory.'[8]

The next morning there was another delegation from Chief Samu inviting Tippu Tip and a few followers to go back and select the tusks they wanted. There was only one condition. All weapons had to be left behind.

It was all too suspicious. Tippu Tip selected twenty Arabs, including his uncle Bushiri, and ten of his best slaves, ordered them to hide guns under their robes and followed the messengers to the village. No sooner were the gates closed behind them than arrows and spears started flying in all directions. Tippu Tip was leading the party and he was immediately wounded. Another Arab and two slaves were killed before Tippu Tip and the rest of his party had time to pull out their guns from under the long white robes, but now they were shooting at close range into the tightly packed crowd, and the screaming villagers fell by the dozen but kept coming at them. 'Our guns were loaded with bullets and buckshot,' Tippu Tip says.[9] 'The *washenzi* were standing together like a flock of birds and they died like birds.' Then suddenly they panicked and fled, leaving behind dead and wounded and trampled children. Within an hour of the start of the fight, they ran out of the village carrying their old fat chief with them.

Tippu Tip had lost a lot of blood and he was in great pain, but he very much enjoyed the sight of the old fat chief being bounced over the heads of his subjects. The only people left behind were the blind and the maimed. 'He was very violent this man,' Tippu Tip says. 'Some offenders had their eyes taken out, others had their noses and hands cut off.'

[8] Murjebi Family Papers.
[9] *Maisha ya Hamed bin Muhammed el Murjebi, yaani Tippu Tip.*

39

He sent for the rest of the caravan and the goods and decided they would spend the night in the village. From the stockades they could see the warriors returning and surrounding the village. Thousands of them, their numbers increasing by the hour with the arrival of Samu's subjects from the outlying villages. Confident in their overwhelming numbers, they sat around the fires beating drums and smoking bhang and tobacco.

Tippu Tip was lying in the chief's *tembe*, and whilst the women attended to his wounds, he was working out a strategy with his uncle and the other Arabs. He decided to station ten men by each of the five village gates. 'When it's dark they will not see us because of the fires,' he instructed them. 'Then shoot into the crowds, and don't stop shooting until they run.'[10] Again because they were standing so close together, the warriors fell by the hundreds.

The next morning the Arabs counted six hundred victims and countless bows and arrows, spears, drums and axes. The rest of the force had fled; but a few hours later they were back again, this time cautiously approaching their village. The Arabs let them come close to the stockade and then opened fire again. Once more the Africans took to their heels and left one hundred and fifty dead behind. It was daylight and the Arabs gave chase. They returned after a few hours having lost two men, and waited for the next attack. When it came, with a much stronger force than the previous day, the Africans lost two hundred and fifty men and the Arabs three. In three days Samu had lost two thousand men, which he could well afford, but although Tippu Tip had only lost seven, they were seven of his best men and irreplaceable, quite apart from the great quantity of gun powder used.

Cut off from the nearest source of supplies and man-power by hundreds of miles of enemy country and with a force of exhausted men, he decided to stay put for a while. Besides, he had no intention of leaving all that ivory in Samu's store, and to move the ivory he needed strong men.

They stayed in the village for a month, but the Africans had given up fighting. Now the only problem was the ivory, and Tippu Tip realised that transporting the huge stock through enemy country, could mean the complete destruction of his caravan.

[10] Murjebi Family Papers.

A council was held and even the slaves were asked for their opinion. A decision was reached and a large armed party went off to look for Samu's scattered armies, leaving Tippu Tip and twenty armed men to hold the village. His uncle Bushiri had insisted he stay behind. His wounds were not healed and many of them were festering after the arrow heads had been dug out of his flesh. A concoction of boiled roots, leaves and sheep's fat had not helped very much, and neither the Arabs nor the Africans knew of other remedies.

As the majority of his men, under his uncle's command, disappeared over the hill, Tippu Tip immediately regretted having agreed to staying behind, and the whole day he limped around the village like a caged leopard. As the day progressed his initial foreboding grew into certainty of disaster and by the time night and darkness came, he was very frightened. For the first and last time he admits that he knew real fear.

Suddenly, coming from the top of the hill, he heard drums and rifle shots and the scouts came running into the village. The rest of the party soon followed jubilantly leading in a thousand prisoners and two thousand goats. The relief was so great that Tippu Tip forgot his limp and ran to meet the returning party. The goats were a tremendous boost and the difference between starvation and a chance to make his way back to Tabora. The two thousand prisoners were also a very welcome bonus, but he suddenly realised that they were all very small men and women. 'Where did you get these from?' he asked his uncle. [11]

'In one of Samu's villages. They were his brother's slaves. I don't know where they come from.'

'Well, they'll be useful for carrying the ivory, I suppose, but I've never seen such small people before.'

The returning party brought him news of sixty *wangwana* [12] who had been killed by Samu's fleeing troops. 'They were traders following in your tracks,' his uncle said. 'They heard of Samu's ivory and our victory, and they must have thought it was safe to follow us. They were all butchered.'

'Well, I'm sure Samu won't try any more tricks with us. We had better start moving.' [13]

Two days later the caravan cautiously filed out of the village,

[11] Murjebi Family Papers.
[12] Freed slaves from the coast of Zanzibar.
[13] Murjebi Family Papers.

headed by Tippu Tip and stretching for a mile behind him. The slaves, the porters and even the guards had to carry loads. There was sixty thousand pounds of ivory in Samu's store, plus twenty four thousand pounds of Katanga copper, salt and assorted provisions.

At first they moved carefully and ready for attack, but it soon became evident that the country was terrified of them. Wherever they passed, the chiefs came out to welcome them, offering gifts and hospitality.

In Urungu, Chief Chungu was delighted to see Tippu Tip. He personally met the caravan at the head of his court musicians and dancers, and led them to a shady spot near water. 'I am happy you defeated Samu,' he said to Tippu Tip. [13] 'He was my enemy and rival. He was a treacherous man. We used to be friends, and I helped him fight many of his enemies, but when I needed his help, he stole three hundred tusks from me and many of my women. That was long ago, but I haven't forgotten. Now you have come and you are my friend. Stay in my country and we will fight Samu together. His country is very big, even if you travel for four months you will not come to the end of it, but now that you and I are friends I will help you finish his whole country, and even punish him for the *wangwana* he killed. I even know the place where they were killed.'

Tippu Tip smiled throughout the long speech and realised that, having defeated the most powerful chief in the area, he would have no further trouble. The others would pay tribute to him and he was more than happy to make friends.

He didn't know it then, but defeating Samu meant that he had started a whole chain of events and a pattern that would repeat itself until the end of his career. Defeat the strongest chief and the rest would fall into his pocket, he thought.

Nevertheless, there was still one thing to do. Samu had to be taught a lasting lesson.

For two months Tippu Tip's caravan camped in Chungu's territory and punitive parties were sent out looking for Samu and his men. According to Tippu Tip this was the time he was given his nick-name because his guns went 'tiptip, in a manner too terrible to hear'. Livingstone, who was in the region at that time, says the name meant 'the gatherer of wealth', [14] but there is no such word in Swahili or the local language.

[14] See Pg. xii.

42

Some of Tippu Tip's men, when out looking for Samu, had come across Livingstone. The missionary doctor was then on his last journey which he had started in the early part of 1866 from Zanzibar. Livingstone was by then a very sick man and very low on provisions. He only had ten porters with him, the others having deserted with his medical supplies and provisions. On the 29th of July, 1867, he recorded his first meeting with Tippu Tip near the village of Ponda south west of Lake Tanganyika.

The missionary was very much impressed by Tippu Tip and his good manners. He was the first European to meet the Arab trader in the interior, and he wrote: 'He presented a goat, a piece of white calico, and four big bunches of beads, also a bag of Holcus sorghum, and apologised because it was so little. He had lost much by Nsama; [15] and received two arrow wounds there.'

Tippu Tip on the other hand, described the explorer as a big Englishman who had neither goods nor rations, and although he couldn't understand the white man's purpose in travelling around like a lost pauper, taking measurements, asking a lot of unimportant questions and always writing in a 'big book'; he immediately offered help and hospitality. He considered 'old Daud', as he called him, just a harmless eccentric whose mania for arguing against the slave trade was to be humoured as just another *desturi ya Wazungu*. [16] Besides he was an old man [17] and very sick, and he had no idea how to keep his followers in order.

This friendliness, almost amounting to infatuation for Europeans, and the wish to be useful to them, was an odd quirk which Tippu Tip retained all his life, despite the fact that some Europeans, and particularly Stanley, didn't treat him very well, and eventually it was Europeans who deprived him of all he had lived for.

Livingstone was very grateful for the slaver's generosity and in his 'big book' he noted that Tippu Tip had lost more in the long fight against Samu than he liked to admit. 'The Arabs had only twenty guns at the time,' Livingstone wrote, 'but some were in the stockade, and though the people of Nsama were very numerous they beat them off, and they fled carrying the bloated carcass of Nsama with them.'

[15] Samu. David Livingstone's *Last Journals*, 1875.
[16] European custom. Anything the Europeans did which was beyond comprehension, was explained as the 'way or the custom of the Europeans'.
[17] At that time Livingstone was only fifty-four-years old.

Livingstone's attempts at leaving the area were frustrated by the war still going on between the Arabs and Samu, but eventually Tippu Tip gave him provisions and guides to take him to Lake Mweru and back. Karambo, another chief in the area, invited Livingstone to stay in his village as a protection against the Arabs.

One of Tippu Tip's men had bought a slave at Karambo's village but the slave had run away. 'Whereupon the Arabs went to Karambo and demanded payment from the chief,' Livingstone wrote. [18] 'He offered clothing, but they refused it, and would have a man. He then offered a man, but this man having two children, they demanded all three. They bully as much as they please by their firearms. After being spoken to by my people the Arabs came away. The chief begged that I would come and visit him once more, for only one day, but it is impossible, for we expect to move directly. My people saw others ... taking fowls and food without payment. Slavery makes a bad neighbourhood .... Slaves are sold here in the same open way that the business is carried on in Zanzibar slave-market. A man goes about calling out the price he wants for the slave, who walks behind him; if a woman, she is taken into a hut to be examined in a state of nudity.... Slavery is a great evil wherever I have seen it. A poor woman and child are among the captives, the boy about three years old seems a mother's pet. His feet are sore from walking in the sun. He was offered for two fathoms, and his mother for one fathom; he understood it all, and cried bitterly, clinging to his mother. She had, of course, no power to help him; they were separated at Karungu.... The above is an episode of every-day occurrence in the wake of the slave-dealer. Two fathoms, mentioned as the price of the boy's life—the more valuable of the two, means four yards of unbleached calico, which is a universal article of barter throughout the greater part of Africa; the mother was bought for two yards. The reader must not think that there are no lower prices; in the famines which succeed the slave-dealer's raid, boys and girls are at times to be purchased for a few handfuls of maize.'

Tippu Tip and his men were not merely fighting or recovering from the long battle, they were also trading as they always did. The whole purpose of fighting *was* collecting more slaves and ivory, and they were glad to be rid of 'old Daud' for a while.

[18] David Livingstone's *Last Journals*.

44

By the time Livingstone had come back from Lake Mweru with his 'great book and measurements', Tippu Tip had agreed to make peace with the old chief in exchange for more ivory and slaves, and the caravan moved on with Livingstone in tow.

The explorer travelled with Tippu Tip's caravan for three months and he wrote: 'Went three hours west of Hara, and came to Nsama's new stockade, built close by the old one burned by Tipo Tipo.... The entire population of the country has received a shock from the conquest of Nsama, and their views of the comparative values of bows and arrows and guns have undergone a great change. Nsama was the Napoleon of these countries; no one could stand before him, hence the defeat of the invincible Nsama has caused a great panic.'

Despite his revulsion for the slavers' methods, Livingstone cannot say enough for the Arabs' politeness and kindness to him, although he often complained of their mode of travel. Their marches were either too long or too short, and they were always being detained to barter for food, slaves or 'some Mohammedan reason'. 'Each party has a guide with a flag,' he says. 'They hasten on with their loads, and hurry with the sheds they build, [19] the masters only bringing up the rear, and helping anyone who may be sick.[20] The distances travelled were quite as much as the masters or we could bear. Had frequent halts been made—as, for instance, a half or a quarter of an hour at the end of every hour or two—but little distress would have been felt: but five hours at a stretch is more than man can bear in a hot climate. The female slaves held on bravely; nearly all carried loads on their heads. The head, or lady of the party, who is also the wife of the Arab, was the only exception. She had a fine white shawl, with ornaments of gold and silver on her head. These ladies had a jaunty walk, and never gave in on the longest march; many pounds' weight of fine copper leglets above the ankles seemed only to help the sway of their walk. As soon as they arrived at the sleeping-place they begin to cook, and in this art they show a good deal of expertness, making savoury dishes for their masters out of wild fruits and other not very likely materials.'

[19] Everytime the caravans stopped, the slaves were herded together in a hastily built compound. Livingstone once saw eighty-five slaves, mostly children of about eight, in this kind of pen.

[20] Tippu Tip in fact walked with Livingstone who was sick, to make sure his guest was properly looked after. He also shortened the daily marching hours in deference to 'old Daud'.

The Arabs always had their concubines travelling with them, and these girls were great favourites. To be chosen as a concubine was an honour, and certainly much better than being an ordinary slave, therefore, these women were more than anxious to please their masters.

At the next stop Tippu Tip decided to send some of his men to the Cazembe of Runda [21] (Samu's neighbour and traditional enemy) to buy ivory. One of his relatives, Mohammed bin Sali, had lived at the court of the Cazembes for ten years and as Livingstone wanted to visit that region, Tippu Tip sent word of the important visitor to his relation. 'One Livingstone will be arriving,' he wrote to the influential man. 'Respect him and do not give him any trouble.'

'I was conveyed by all the Arabs for some distance,' Livingstone wrote. [22] 'They have been extremely kind.'

And so Tippu Tip parted from 'old Daud', having given him guides 'to take him to other places and wherever he wanted to go', provisions and a promise to send some of his belongings to Ujiji to await his arrival. 'Our business was finished,' Tippu Tip says, 'and we started the journey back to the coast.'

On the return journey they visited Samu, in his newly reconstructed village, to show there were no hard feelings, but the old chief refused to see Tippu Tip and only agreed to receive a few of his representatives to convey their leader's greetings. Tippu Tip laughed at the chief's surliness, and he could well afford to laugh. The inhabitants of the whole region paid tribute to him and the minor chiefs of the area went out of their way to be friendly. Obtaining porters and supplies was no problem now, as each regional chief offered all Tippu Tip asked for and more.

Tabora was hundreds of miles out of his way, but distance and time meant nothing to Tippu Tip and he decided to visit his father and recruit fresh Wanyamwezi porters. Tabora was almost deserted of Arabs. They were away fighting Chief Mkasiwa. The same Mkasiwa they had fought for and elected chief only a few years before. He was glad to hear that his father was not involved this time; he was away trading, but Karunde welcomed him as always. The Arabs were anxious to enlist his help again, but he told them he had no intention of getting involved in their

[21] Cazembe of Runda has been spelt in many different ways by writers of the period: Kasembe of Lunda, Casembe and Kazembe.
[22] David Livingstone's *Last Journals*.

skirmishes, and after two months he reassembled his caravan and proceeded to the coast.

There was only one more stop to make. On his way to Lake Tanganyika he had left an agent with 6,000 dollars' worth of barter goods to trade with a minor chief, and now he wanted to pick up the profits. Unfortunately, all the agent could show for his years of trading was two slave girls. Tippu Tip was furious. He locked the man up for four days and then released him. 'The man who hits himself, does not cry!' he told Professor Brode many years later in the way of an explanation.

In view of the enormous caravan of ivory and slaves he was bringing back to the coast, he could well afford the loss of 6,000 dollars.

CHAPTER SIX

Zanzibar and Glory

The unstable Sultan Majid had never felt safe in Zanzibar. Through British intervention his rebellious brother Barghash had been allowed back into Zanzibar, and Majid felt he had to have 'a harbour of peace' away from the island and the affairs of state —quite apart from the continual British pressure over the slave question. Majid found exactly what he needed on the mainland, about forty-five miles south of Zanzibar, the perfect spot with a good harbour and plenty of 'sweet water'. He called it Dar es Salaam, or harbour of peace, and in 1866 he set about building and personally supervising the erection of a palace, a fort and quarters for his retinue. All building materials had to be brought in at great expense, and a steam-tug was ordered from Hamburg to lead the ships into the harbour through the narrow inlet. [1] He offered free land to all who were prepared to cultivate it, but this new whim of the Sultan was not very popular with the people of Zanzibar. One of the main objections was the possibility of escape for the slaves. At the very beginning of the project, forty of the Sultan's personal slaves escaped. Being on the mainland, Dar es Salaam offered a perfect opportunity for slaves to try and reach their country of origin.

Majid became irrationally angry if anybody suggested that Dar es Salaam was not an excellent idea. He went as far as having people flogged for disagreeing with him, and his plan went ahead. New caravan routes were planned to Kilwa in the south, and Lamu in the north, [2] and messengers were sent out to inform traders of the new port.

[1] German officers and engineers ran the Sultan's fleet.
[2] From Cape Delgado in the south to Warsheikh in the north, the East African coast was under the Sultan's jurisdiction.

Tippu Tip's caravan was the first to arrive in Dar es Salaam since the Sultan had started the project, and the Sultan's court was in residence. 'Everybody was there,' Tippu Tip says. Leading Arabs and Swahilis from Zanzibar, Lamu, Pemba and Mombasa; consuls and foreign business men; Banyans and Indians, and among the latter, those who had financed Tippu Tip's caravan when it left for the interior six years before.

It was the 22nd of the month of Ramadhan, and Tippu Tip ordered his caravan to halt outside Dar es Salaam and 'clean up' before the grand entrance into the new town the following day.

Despite the strict fasting of Ramadhan, there was great excitement in Dar es Salaam when the enormous caravan marched in, beating drums, firing guns and blowing conch shells. Not only the Indian creditors, but the whole population of Zanzibar would benefit by Tippu Tip's good fortune, and from the Sultan to the most miserable of the traders, they all welcomed Tippu Tip as a hero.

'The end of Ramadhan is at hand, Hamed,' Sultan Majid said to Tippu Tip. [3] 'I want you to stay here and celebrate it with us. It will be a greater feast than ever now that you are back.'

Tippu Tip was in a hurry to get back to Zanzibar with his ivory and slaves, but Majid didn't like opposition. 'We have seen your ivory and your people. Now send them to Zanzibar. You will stay here for the feast and when it's over you will travel back to Zanzibar with me,' the Sultan ordered and Tippu Tip obeyed.

This was, of course, a great honour. Many years had passed since he had been just another Zanzibar trader 'with neither goods nor reputation', as he put it, and even more years had passed since, as a child, he had dreamt of being acclaimed a hero by his Sultan and the people of Zanzibar.

When the time came to sail from Dar es Salaam, much to the British Consul's annoyance, the Sultan boarded a French ship. [4] His court and his most important guests, including Tippu Tip, sailed on the Sultan's launches, followed by a flotilla of smaller vessels and dhows. The boats were extravagantly decorated with flags and buntings and the sailors were dressed in the scarlet

[3] Murjebi Family Papers.
[4] The Sultan's fleet included British built frigates and corvettes, four steam-ships and two steam-launches.

49

and gold uniforms of the Sultan's household. A splendid home-coming for a slaver.

For six months after his arrival, Tippu Tip was busy with the sale of ivory and slaves, and one day he was summoned to the Sultan's palace. To his surprise Majid enquired about his plans for future expeditions and then announced that he would arrange for Set Ladda, the Indian in charge of his Customs, to give Tippu Tip all the goods he wanted—on credit. This placed the trader in a rather awkward position as he had already arranged for Taria Topan, another Indian and one of the most powerful bankers in Zanzibar,[5] to give him all the credit he needed. In Tippu Tip's customary non-plussed manner, he merely accepted goods from both and for a year continued making preparations and enjoying the fruits of his efforts. He prepared the loads, engaged the porters, sent them off to his father in Tabora, and then set about arranging for the most important item of any expedition to be assembled and shipped—gunpowder. He bought 5,000 dollars' worth of English gunpowder and stored it in his newly acquired town house, ready for shipment to the mainland.

Unfortunately for him, his house was next door to the British Consulate and one night he was woken up by loud banging on his front door. Two messengers from the Sultan's palace informed him that he was ordered to report to the Sultan's chief adviser.

Having presented himself he was asked if he was storing gunpowder in the house next to the consulate. 'Yes, I am. What of it?' he replied. 'Are you crazy?' the adviser asked. 'No, my brain is still intact.' Tippu Tip replied. 'Don't you know that gunpowder cannot be stored in the town?' 'No, I didn't know that. I didn't know about any law that said gunpowder couldn't be stored in a man's own house—even if it *is* next door to the British Consulate.'[6]

The exasperated adviser finally sent Tippu Tip home but told him to report again the next day to hear the verdict.

The Sultan was extremely sorry, the adviser told him the following day. He had no idea the culprit would be his friend Hamed bin Muhammed el Murjebi, but the consul had to be kept happy and therefore it had been decided that Tippu Tip could either pay a fine or go to jail for a few days. He chose

[5] Later made Sir Taria by the British.
[6] Murjebi Family Papers.

the jail sentence. 'Anyway, I was given a good room,' he says. 'My servants came with food and even my women slept there.' After two days he was released and he went immediately to pay a visit to Consul Kirk.

'I haven't seen you for days, Hamed,' the Consul said.

'That's right,' Tippu Tip replied. 'I was in jail about this gunpowder business.'

'I didn't know it was you, Hamed, I am sorry. I thought one of your servants or assistants ...' he continued lamely.

'Ah, servants and assistants. Mine always do what I tell them. No, no it was me. Don't worry. I didn't mind going to jail at all. I wanted to know what it was like and I enjoyed the whole thing,' he laughed and blinked. [6] The Consul apologised again. After all Tippu Tip had helped his friend Dr. Livingstone [7] and was rapidly becoming a very influential man, both in Zanzibar and on the mainland.

On the other hand, Tippu Tip really enjoyed the whole thing, but not for the reasons given. He was a snob and he very much liked the idea of having Sultans and British Consuls apologising to him. However, he felt no resentment towards Dr. Kirk or the Sultan and before leaving on his next expedition, he made a special trip to Dar es Salaam to pay his respects to Majid who was hiding again in his Harbour of Peace. This time for good reason. Cholera was raging again in Zanzibar and people were dying by the hundreds. Anybody who could, left the island, or at least took refuge in the countryside.

Tippu Tip had moved his whole household to Kwarara, his mother's property where he was born, but even so the disease attacked and decimated. His mother begged him to leave and save himself. 'You have a great responsibility Hamed. Your brothers, your uncles, your cousins and all your followers are waiting for you to take them out of Zanzibar. Take them out, my son, and I will take care of your wife and children here.' [8]

He hadn't even left Bagamoyo when news of his mother's death reached him. There was nothing he could do now; he had to go on and reach Tabora before the porters started to die. He was carrying 50,000 dollars' worth of Indian capital and he couldn't afford to lose it, but despite his efforts to leave the

[7] From 1858 to 1863 Dr. John Kirk had served as surgeon and botanist on David Livingstone's expedition to the Zambesi.

[8] Murjebi Family Papers.

'coast sickness' behind, the porters died. They died by the dozen. 'Everyday they died,' Tippu Tip says and more loads had to be discarded. They dug great pits along the route and buried the most precious loads, but men kept dying, and more loads had to be buried. Word of the 'coast sickness' had preceded them and it became increasingly difficult to get food. Nobody would come near them to sell, and they were too weak to fight for it.

Wagogo warriors were blocking their path. 'You will not go near our villages,' they ordered. 'You will go through the bush or we'll kill you,' they shouted in a state of great excitement.

'Well, death is death anywhere,' Tippu Tip said to Abdallah, another uncle who had joined him in Zanzibar. 'In the bush we *will* die of cholera and starvation. Here, we *may* die of cholera and a spear through the heart. I would rather risk the spears and cholera in the open, than die in the bush like a hungry rat.' [9]

They all agreed with him and an ultimatum was given to the head warrior to convey to his chief. The Wagogo knew Arab slavers and the power of their guns, so after a lengthy *baraza*, [10] they agreed to sell them food and let them pass. A great relief for the whole caravan.

Tippu Tip had sent couriers to Tabora to warn his father of his difficulties, and soon after leaving Ugogo the old man arrived with fresh porters. It was a sad reunion. Tippu Tip had not seen his father for eight years and the news they exchanged were not happy ones. Tippu Tip told his father of his mother's death, and Muhammed told his son of Karunde's death. 'She was a good wife, my wife Karunde—and so was your mother,' he added. [9] 'I am an old man now. I need a strong woman to take care of my household, so I have decided to take another of Fundi Kira's daughters. Her name is Nyaso. She is young and strong and she will keep my house in order. She is Karunde's youngest sister, and Karunde liked her. She is a good girl and has brought me many riches. Chief Mkasiwa wanted me to marry one of his daughters, but I don't like him. He's always fighting. The Arabs are having trouble with him now and when they heard you were coming they were very happy. They think you will help them again.'

Tippu Tip was tired of wasting time fighting for the Tabora Arabs. 'They're always having trouble. They're as frightened

[9] Murjebi Family Papers.
[10] Meeting, talk.

52

and timid as a harem full of women, and I've had enough of them. I must go back for the loads we buried and there are far better places than Tabora for me. West of the lake there are riches that no Tabora Arab has ever dreamt of, and the greatest chiefs in the world are begging for me to go back and trade with them. Why should I bother with Tabora?'[11]

Nevertheless, before he could reach this mythical land of submissive chiefs and fabulous wealth, there were quite a number of obstacles to overcome; from famine to unco-operative chiefs, deserting porters and mass poisoning.

Tippu Tip had recruited a whole new lot of Wanyamwezi porters in Tabora, but no sooner had he met trouble with a chief by the name of Riova in Ugalla, than all the porters ran back to Tabora.

Chief Riova was a drunk and his whole village followed his example, but were it not for the fact that one of the drunken villagers speared and killed one of Tippu Tip's favourite women, Riova might have remained in power long after the Arab caravan had passed through his country.

The woman was actually married to one of Tippu Tip's personal slaves, but the master was very fond of her. Her husband, who was known as *Simba*, the lion, because of his bravery in battle, swore revenge and his master fully supported the idea. The whole incident was over in a few hours. Chief Riova was shot trying to escape through a hole at the back of his senior wife's *tembe* and his deposed brother was immediately on hand to sit on the vacant throne. Unfortunately, when it came to counting the dead, the brave Simba was found to be one of them.

The problem of the missing porters was resolved by Tippu Tip's father who rounded them up again and sent them back to his son under armed escort.

At last they were marching again towards the southern end of Lake Tanganyika and through the most desolate country they had ever crossed. Drought, wars and famine had reduced the surviving population to selling themselves for a few handfuls of food—any food, and although Tippu Tip had stocked up in Ugalla, by the time they reached Itawa, his men were starving.

Samu's country had fully recovered from Tippu Tip's previous invasion and before he could do anything about it, the four thousand men in his caravan were gorging themselves on

[11] Murjebi Family Papers.

the first crop they found, bitter uncooked cassava. [12] Within a few hours forty of them had died and the rest were in agonies of vomiting and diarrhoea.

Tippu Tip and his aides tried every remedy they could think of, but nothing seemed to stop the vomiting and diarrhoea. They were desperate when Juma bin Sef who had been sent to test Samu's reactions, came back with gifts of goats and food, grudgingly sent by Samu as tribute. The old chief still refused to see Tippu Tip, but he had agreed to trade with his envoys. Juma and the goats saved the sick men. Juma had had previous experience with bitter cassava. Gallons of broth was made from lean goat meat, red peppers and ginger, and the men were fed this concoction. Those who refused it were forcibly fed and after a few days, they were marching again through Samu's country where people were more than anxious to give them all they wanted.

Tippu Tip was not a man to bear a grudge, especially if a grudge meant loss of business, so he left Samu and his new stores of ivory in his brother Muhammed's capable hands, crossed the river Lunda in full flood and proceeded to explore the legendary land of the Kasembe.

[12] Bitter cassava has to be soaked in cold water for six days until it ferments. Then, when it is white and sweet, it can be cooked and eaten. Cassava (Muhogo in Swahili), is still grown all over East Africa and in village or city streets it is roasted in strips over charcoal fires and sold like hot chestnuts are sold in Europe, but it's not as tasty.

CHAPTER SEVEN

From the Kings of Kasembe to the Cannibals of Utetera

The kingdom of Kasembe was known to Portuguese traders from the Mozambique coast since the 18th century. Livingstone explored the region and lived at the court of Kasembe Maonga, the 7th ruler, after he parted with Tippu Tip in 1867.

'There have been seven Casembes in all,' Livingstone wrote at the time. [1] 'The word means general. The chief's residence is enclosed in a wall of reeds, 8 or 9 ft. high, and 30 yards square. The gateway is ornamented with about sixty human skulls; a shed stands in the middle of the road before we come to the gate, with a cannon dressed in gaudy cloths.... Mohammed Bin Saleh [2] now met us, his men firing guns of welcome; he conducted us to a hut till we could build one of our own. Mohammed is a fine portly black Arab, with a pleasant smile, and pure white beard, and has been more than ten years in these parts, and lived with four Casembes: he has considerable influence here, and also on Tanganyika. An Arab trader, Mohammed Bogharibm who arrived days before us with an immense number of slaves, presented a meal of vermicelli, oil, and honey, also cassava meal cooked, so as to resemble a sweetmeat (I had not tasted honey or sugar since we left Lake Nyassa, in September 1866): they had coffee too.... Many of Casembe's people appear with the ears cropped and hands lopped off: the present chief has been often guilty of this barbarity. One man has just come to us with-

[1] All quotes from David Livingstone in this chapter are from his *Last Journals*.

[2] Tippu Tip's relative who had been instructed to look after Livingstone at Kasembe.

out ears or hands: he tried to excite our pity making a chirruping noise, by striking his cheeks with the stumps of his hands.'

When Livingstone was presented to the Kasembe he found him reclining on lion and leopard skins outside his *tembe*, dressed in a 'crinoline like garment' of brightly coloured stripes and surrounded by his court. The kind missionary found it hard to relax in the presence of the cross-eyed Kasembe, surrounded as they were by the great number of mutilated people.

'His executioner also came forward,' Livingstone noted. 'He had a curious scissor-like instrument at his neck for cropping ears. On saying to him that his was nasty work, he smiled, and so did many who were not sure of their ears a moment.... Casembe's chief wife passes frequently to her plantation, carried by six, or more, commonly twelve men in a sort of palanquin: she had European features, but light brown complexion. A number of men run before her, brandishing swords and battle-axes, and one beats a hollow instrument, giving warning to passengers to clear the way: she has two enormous pipes ready filled for smoking. She is very attentive to her agriculture: cassava is the chief product; sweet potatoes, maize, sorghum, millet, ground-nuts, cotton. The people seem to be more savage than any I have seen: they strike each other barbarously from mere wantonness, but they are civil enough to me.... This part was well stocked with people five years ago, but Casembe's severity in cropping ears and other mutilations, selling the children for slight offences etc., made them all flee to neighbouring tribes; and now if he sent all over the country, he could collect a thousand men....'

Some years had passed since Livingstone's visit to Kasembe. From there he had gone back to Ujiji accompanied by Tippu Tip's relative, and sometimes carried by his slaves when he was too sick to go on; only to find that the stores sent to Ujiji by Kirk, had been stolen. He says the Ujiji traders were 'of the worst kind. Those whom I met in Urungu and Itawa were gentlemen slavers....'

Tippu Tip, Livingstone's gentleman slaver, was now attempting to ford the swollen river which separated Kasembe's Lunda from Itawa. The cross-eyed Kasembe had been deposed and another elected in his place, but the reception his subjects gave Tippu Tip when he finally crossed the river, was no better than he would have expected from the previous Kasembe. A small party of Tippu Tip's people who had gone looking for food, were immediately killed and when explanations were asked, Tippu Tip was told that as the Kasembe and Samu were the most powerful chiefs in that part of the world, and Tippu Tip had already defeated Samu, the Kasembe thought he'd better show the Arabs that they could not deal with him the way they had dealt with Samu. This meant war to Tippu Tip's ears, and war he gave them. Within a month 'we reached Kasembe's village,' he says, [3] 'we killed him, we took his property, many guns, ivory and countless men.'

Having subdued the two most important countries in that region, Kasembe's Lunda and Samu's Itawa, he could now proceed with his *peaceful* trading. No other chief dared oppose him, and from as far as Katanga they sent deputations to meet his advancing caravan with gifts of ivory and slaves, and invitations for Tippu Tip to visit their country. Trading was not brisk but steady, and the caravan swelled with ivory and slaves, and slowly it moved on towards the Lualaba river.

They were approaching the river when messengers arrived from a deposed chief.

'They are always being deposed,' Tippu Tip said to his entourage. [3]

'That is so. Our master Mrongo Tambwe has been deposed again,' the uncomprehending messenger replied.

'Never mind. Tell me about your master,' Tippu Tip said.

Mrongo Tambwe and Mrongo Kasanga were brothers, but since their father's death they had been fighting over their small territory along the swamps of the Lualaba river. Whichever of the two brothers won the day's fight, took over the villages along the swamp, whilst the other retreated into the forest and started getting ready for the next battle. The brother now in the forest and trying to regain his seat, was Mrongo Tambwe, and having heard of Tippu Tip, he had sent messengers with promises of great gains if the powerful Arab and his forces would agree to to help Tambwe defeat his brother.

Tippu Tip accepted the challenge, not out of sympathy for the loser, but because he wanted control of the swamp area which was a great trap for elephants. The people of the swamps drove the elephants to the muddy banks, and when the helpless beasts were stuck in the mud, they were killed by the hundreds.

Tippu Tip describes the swamp as so full of fish that neigh-

[3] Murjebi Family Papers.

57

bouring tribes came for miles to buy it. The fish was very good, he says, and the people of the swamps exchanged it for *viramba*. [4] They needed cloth and their neighbours needed fish, therefore, on market days as many as six thousand people collected on the banks of the swamp to barter. The market was held on *No Man's Land*, and although the different villages might be fighting for the rest of the week, it was an unwritten law that on market days they were all immune from attack. The swamp was the very life of the country, and any one controlling it, controlled the country. Too good an opportunity for Tippu Tip to miss.

Mrongo Kasanga, the brother then in power, also sent messengers to the Arabs to invite them to trade.

'Tell your master that my business is with his brother, and that I consider Tambwe the rightful heir,' Tippu Tip told the messengers. [5]

'Then there will be fighting,' they informed him.

'Then there will be fighting,' Tippu Tip confirmed.

Although the villages stretched for miles and they were surrounded by stockades, Tippu Tip's forces managed to win once again. People ran for their boats to take refuge on the little islands, but large numbers were killed, their villages set alight and four hundred of their women captured.

Mrongo Tambwe was very grateful. He invited his new allies to stay, supplied them with ivory and boat-loads of fish, and assured them of his undying loyalty; which was all that Tippu Tip expected but other markets awaited him.

'There were so many ducks that one barrel would bring down thirty or more,' Tippu Tip says. [6] 'But after nine months of being fed fish and ducks, we'd had enough. We collected the ivory due to us and we were ready to go.'

He was off once again, but first he sent his friend Said bin Ali to trade with Msiri of Katanga. Msiri had repeatedly invited them to come and buy his copper. He had a lot of copper and no cloth. 'And that suits us very well. We will not need cloth where we are going,' Tippu Tip explained to Said. [6] The country they were preparing to explore, with guides supplied by the grateful Mrongo Tambwe, was Irande where the *viramba* cloth was manufactured and where no 'free man' from the coast had ever been.

[4] A cloth made from the bark of trees.
[5] Murjebi Family Papers.   [6] Murjebi Family Papers.

58

They had already crossed the Lualaba river when they heard that another Arab trader was in the country. Juma bin Salum, [7] better known as Juma Merikani as he traded mainly in the white cotton cloth which originally came from America, was an old hand. He had met Burton and Speke in 1858 and had traded beyond Lake Tanganyika for years. He was much older than Tippu Tip and had become more conservative in his old age, but Tippu Tip wanted him to join the caravan for the journey to the unknown country. Although Juma Merikani's camp was two days' march away, Tippu Tip turned back and invited the older trader to go along with them to Irande. 'Not I,' said Juma. [6] 'I've heard that Irande is thick with people, and you don't know what a lot of people will do to newcomers. I'd rather stay here in Urua and collect the little bit of ivory brought to me. Why take risks? I'm happy here.' However, as Tippu Tip had by then collected thousands of pounds of ivory, Juma Merikani agreed to look after it until they returned.

They parted, Juma to stay and quietly trade ivory for merikani, and Tippu Tip to venture into the unknown.

Juma Merikani need not have worried about Irande. The people were the most peaceful and industrious that Tippu Tip had ever come across. They made *viramba* and their whole existence seemed to revolve around the making and the selling of their cloth. Their large villages consisted of neat long rows of huts, like clove plantations, Tippu Tip remarked, and between the rows of huts there was a covered-in place where the viramba makers worked. Tippu Tip was very much impressed by their form of government which was one of the most democratic in the world. They elected a new chief every two years and a council of elders made sure the people received a fair share from the sale of the cloth. They also had a very novel way of paying a dead man's debts. The family merely hung the body from a tree and his possessions were laid out on the ground for the creditors to help themselves.

All this was most interesting, but Irande lacked the only thing Tippu Tip was really interested in—ivory. He didn't see a single tusk nor any elephants, so he peacefully passed on to the next region, leaving the Irande people to the manufacture of bark cloth and the belief that guns were a strange kind of 'pestle' for crushing maize. Tippu Tip was charmed by these peace loving

[7] Also spelt Saleh by Prof. Brode.

59

people and their orderly way of life. So much so that he didn't even attempt to steal a few women. A feeling not shared by one of his lieutenants many years later when he invaded the country and left it poor and bleeding. The explorer Herman Wissman passed through Irande soon after this event and he was shocked by the devastation.

That catastrophe was not to overtake the peaceful viramba makers for many years and Tippu Tip had left them with their illusions. He marched for months, passing through one small chiefdom after another, and everywhere the small chiefs were either fighting each other, or fighting aspiring chiefs within their own country, or deposed chiefs, or just friends and relations. One such deposed chief, unjustly so he claimed, was Pange Bondo.

Pange Bondo one day appeared at Tippu Tip's camp with a gift of four ivory tusks and asked for Tippu Tip's friendship.

'I will be your friend,' Tippu Tip replied graciously accepting the tusks. [8]

The story was simple. Even though a man may be born hereditary chief of that territory, he will only be allowed to stay in office for two—at the most, three years. When Pange Bondo's term of office came to an end, he didn't feel like retiring. 'I liked my work very much,' he explained. 'But they threw me out and even my children are deprived of their right to rule. The chieftainship has been passed to another family altogether.'

'That's disgraceful,' Tippu Tip laughed. 'But what can I do about it?'

'Lend me the voice of your guns. The people will listen to sense,' he said squatting down next to his host. Tippu Tip's followers were shocked. Nobody sat uninvited on the master's carpet, much less a dirty infidel. Tippu Tip had established a strict discipline of rank and status at the very beginning of his career, and except for his relations, nobody entered his tent uninvited. Now they waited for his well known shout of command, but Tippu Tip liked Pange Bondo.

'But he is a rogue,' his uncle Bushiri remonstrated.

'I like rogues, especially funny rogues, and this one amuses me,' he said in Arabic. [9] 'Well, chief, all right I will help you. But not just yet. I have urgent business to attend to first, but

[8] Murjebi Family Papers.
[9] Murjebi Family Papers.

I will come back and make you chief again as soon as I have finished my business.'

Pange Bondo was delighted and he left, promising eternal friendship.

Tippu Tip's urgent business entailed another move. Urua was a poor country and he decided it was time to leave and explore the country immediately ahead. He had heard that Utetera [10] was teaming with elephants and that 'the people were very stupid'. Just the right combination for some brisk business.

Utetera was a huge country and thickly populated, but because of their 'stupidity' the inhabitants were always being attacked by their neighbours and with each defeat they became more and more timid. They were, in other words, at everybody's mercy, and the last chief to beat them in battle, and latest tyrant, now blocked Tippu Tip's advance into the country. Utetera paid taxes to him, he said, and if Tippu Tip wanted permission to go through he would have to pay. Tippu Tip was accustomed to paying *hongo*, and even extortionists' hongo, but what this chief was asking was the highest he had ever been asked. Thirty lengths of cloth and seventy pounds of beads. An unheard of entrance fee, but he paid, reserving himself the pleasure of retribution for another time. Important business lay ahead, but no sooner had he paid the extortionist, than another party came to him and proposed a joint attack on the 'timid' people. The rewards sounded inviting —ivory and slaves for all, but he had already made up his mind as to his course of action with the Watetera, and he declined the offer of a partner.

His plan had barely matured in his mind, when messengers arrived from Utetera inviting him to come and trade in their country. This invitation he accepted with pleasure as it so well coincided with his own plan.

Tippu Tip had taken the trouble of finding out all he could about Chief Kasongo Rushie of the Watetera. One of his girls was from this very country and he had learnt many things since the day he had bought her. Sex was not the only thing he demanded from his women. The girl had told him that many years before two of Chief Kasongo's favourite sisters were sold into slavery and nobody had heard another thing about the princesses of Utetera. However, this was not the story Tippu Tip told Chief Kasongo's messengers. He told them that one of the princesses

[10] Sometimes spelt Utetela.

had been sold to his own grand-father in Zanzibar, and she had become his favourite concubine. From this happy union Tippu Tip's mother was born. His colour and features helped a great deal in making the story credible, also a few words of their language which he had learnt from his slave girl, went a long way to convince the envoys of the authenticity of this fantastic story.

'My grandmother, the enslaved princess, always told me about the beauty and the wealth of your land,' he said [11] to the messengers as they shared a large platter of rice and mutton set out on mats in front of his tent. 'She always spoke about Utetera and although she was treated like an Arab wife, she longed to see her country again. She never did, but just before she died she made me promise that one day I would come here and find her brother, your honoured chief. It has taken long years, and as you know, many battles for me to reach this land, but now I am here and soon I shall see my great-uncle, your honoured Chief Kasongo Rushie.' The messengers were convinced. They looked from Tippu Tip to the other Arabs, and they all nodded.

'You will see him soon. We shall return in a few days with a proper escort for the son of a princess.'

Unfortunately the neighbours who had invited Tippu Tip to join them against the Watetera [12] believed the meeting to be against their interest, so without asking for explanations, they started beating on their war drums, and before the Arabs could ask any questions, they were surrounded and fighting.

Somehow the deposed chief Pange Bondo managed to sneak into the Arab camp after a few hours of fighting.

'What do you want now, Pange?' Tippu Tip asked when the smiling African was brought to him. [13] 'Can't you see I'm busy?'

'I can help you stop this useless fighting. These washenzi are no use to you.'

'What makes you think that? We've already captured a thousand women and their goats.'

'Ah, that's nothing compared to Utetera where your uncle is waiting. I know about that. Pange knows everything. You make me chief again, and I will help you.'

'All right. I will see that you are made chief again,' Tippu

[11] Murjebi Family Papers.
[12] *Wa*tetera, Swahili plural for *U*tetera.
[13] Murjebi Family Papers.

Tip laughed. 'Now tell me how you are going to stop the fighting.'

'It's easy. If you agree to return the prisoners, they will agree to stop fighting.'

'Never.'

'But you don't really have to return them. I will tell them that you agree to return all the prisoners who were born here. Anybody else, you keep. Most of the women are Watetera anyway and I will point them out to you. Then you can go and make a present of them to your uncle. He will be pleased and you will make me chief again. There's just one more thing. These people don't know about guns. They will ask you to revive the people you killed. They think they've fainted at the sound of thunder from your sticks.'

'I can't revive the dead.'

'Yes you can—well, they will think you can. You say a few words in your language and then tell them that in ten days the sleeping people will get up again.'

The peace negotiations were successfully carried out as Pange had predicted and all Tippu Tip had to do to show his gratitude was present himself with his troops at Pange's village and the age-old traditions were immediately reversed. Pange Bondo was re-elected chief and his newly found friend witnessed the coronation ceremony.

It was a colourful affair. First of all wet clay was plastered all over Pange's head, then a split basket was placed over the wet clay and finally ten small live chicks were strung round his neck. These ornaments had to remain in place for ten days, despite the fact that the chicks would die in a much shorter time.

Tippu Tip had enjoyed playing fairy-godmother to his resourceful friend, but the time had come to part company and enter the promised land of Utetera and 'uncle' Kasongo.

CHAPTER EIGHT

Uncle Kasongo and
Lt. Cameron, R.N.

'Uncle' Kasongo had sent envoys to lead Tippu Tip and his enormous caravan into the heart of Utetera. The messengers had told
the chief the amazing story of his sister's grandchild and Kasongo
quickly realised that this was one nephew he had better acknowledge. Besides with Tippu Tip's fighting force and reputation,
no neighbour would dare bother Kasongo again. To show his
pleasure at the prospect of meeting Tippu Tip, he sent three
hundred goats and twenty large elephant tusks.

Accompanied by the envoys and a member of Kasongo's royal
clan, they travelled for days studying the country they crossed,
Tippu Tip congratulating himself on his choice of uncles. Utetera
would suit him very well for a few years.

Kasongo had prepared a great reception for them. Thousands
of people came to meet them when they approached the chief's
village. Banana leaf arches were erected all along the road leading
to the village specially prepared for them and close to Kasongo's.
Women brought baskets of fruit and vegetables. A herd of goats
was led into a compound for their use and slaves were handed
over to them. Kasongo's chief adviser, a very old man almost
completely covered in monkey skins, welcomed them into the
village. 'My master will visit you after you have eaten and re-
freshed yourself,' he said bowing to Tippu Tip. [1]

Chief Kasongo didn't let him wait too long. Drumming and
blowing of horns announced his arrival and the Arabs were ready
to receive him in their best white *lungi*, gold embroidered coats
and ceremonial head dress. Greetings were exchanged and then

[1] Murjebi Family Papers.

the old chief and Tippu Tip alone entered the *baraza* and discussed the future of Utetera. When they finally emerged, they were both smiling and the people stamped and screamed with pleasure.

'Tomorrow we will have a great baraza in my village and my people will hear what I propose,' he said vigorously shaking Tippu Tip's hands. [1]

What Chief Kasongo Rushie proposed was all that Tippu Tip could wish for and more. The chief told his people that he was getting old and tired and he could no longer fight his enemies alone. Now a man, not a stranger, but the grandson of his sister, had come from very far away to give him the power of his youth and strength. 'Obey him,' he said. [1] 'As I am chief, he is chief with me. For protecting us against our enemies he will only ask for the teeth of the elephant. Give them to him, and all that he requires.'

Fortunately for Tippu Tip, Chief Kasongo believed that the Elephant was the chief of the animals in the same way that the Sun was the chief of the skies. Therefore he never looked at the sun nor did he ever touch an elephant tusk.

Life in Kasongo settled down into a simple routine of peaceful trading and punitive parties against offending neighbours. He was fair with his new subjects but pitiless against offenders, and his punitive parties spread terror around the countryside.

One such punitive party, sixty men led by his uncle Bushiri, was ambushed and every single member of the party was killed and eaten on the spot. When news of his uncle's death reached him in Kasongo's capital, Tippu Tip was furious and very sad. Uncle Bushiri was closer to him than his own father, and although Tippu Tip never killed for the sake of killing, this time he led his own forces and allowed them to butcher and eat the enemy until the smell of flesh made him sick. Chief Kasongo had gone with him and brought his own army, and for days they hunted, looted, burnt and killed.

Most of the regions Tippu Tip had crossed, from the time he had approached Samu's kingdom, indulged in cannibalism. When Livingstone met Tippu Tip in Itawa, Samu's territory, he noticed that although 'the women excited the admiration of the Arabs because of their fine, small, well-formed features : their defect is one of fashion,' he wrote. [2] 'They file their teeth to points, the

[2] David Livingstone's *Last Journals*.

65

hussies, and that makes their smile like that of the crocodile.' The only time Livingstone allowed his followers to shoot was when he had been repeatedly attacked by cannibals and there was no other means of escape.

Despite their eating habits, the Watetera made good loyal subjects, and their neighbours, after being defeated in a series of battles, contributed their quota of ivory, goats and slaves. Pange Bondo was one of the most loyal contributors to Tippu Tip's stores. For the next three years every chief in the neighbourhood, anxious to please and have the friendship of Kasongo's powerful ally, received Tippu Tip's 'scouting' parties with 'great respect', and sent ivory, slaves and food without question.

Whatever his faults, Tippu Tip never failed to support the chiefs who paid for his friendship and protection. One of these chiefs was Rusuna who complained to Tippu Tip that the Arabs of Nyangwe, on the Lualaba/Congo river, kept sending raiding parties into his territory.

'You mean there are Arabs now at Nyangwe?'

'A great settlement of Ujiji Arabs, Sultan,' Chief Rusuna replied. 'Will you protect us against them, even if they are coast people and brothers to you?' [3]

Tippu Tip was delighted. Ten years had passed since he had encircled Lake Tanganyika and been in contact with other Arabs from the coast, and as his gun-smith had recently died, he decided to pay a visit to his compatriots at Nyangwe and have his guns repaired at the same time.

Another visitor had arrived at Nyangwe a few weeks before. In 1873, Verney Lovett Cameron, an English naval officer, had been sent to Zanzibar by the Geographical Society to organise an expedition to assist Livingstone who was again in trouble after Stanley's visit. By the time Cameron arrived in Tabora, Livingstone's body was being carried back to the coast by his servants Chuma and Susi who had remained with him to the last. The only other two Englishmen [4] in Cameron's expedition joined the small group travelling to Zanzibar, and Cameron went on to Ujiji and the exploration of the area beyond Lake Tanganyika. He finally arrived at Nyangwe and for weeks he tried to buy canoes to take him and his two hundred men down the Lualaba

[3] Murjebi Family Papers.
[4] Lt. Murphy and Dr. Dillan who died within a few days of leaving Cameron.

and the river he felt must be the great Congo river.

When Tippu Tip arrived in August 1874, Cameron was still waiting to buy canoes, but he found that cowries, goats and slaves were the only currency acceptable to the people of Nyangwe, and of these commodities the explorer had none. He managed to barter some of his supplies for cowrie shells, but even so the local boat owners and builders refused to sell to him. One boat owner explained that if he took cowries home, his wives would only waste them on ornaments for themselves and he would be short of a boat. When Cameron offered to double the quantity so that the wives could be satisfied and the man could barter with the others, the African explained that it was much simpler if Cameron went off to the market and exchanged the cowries for slaves, and then paid for the boat with the slaves.

Behind this lack of co-operation with the explorer was the Swahili headman, Mwinyi Dugumbi, 'who, finding himself a far greater personage here than he could ever hope to be in his native place, gave up all idea of returning to the coast, and devoted his attention and energies to establishing a harem,' Cameron wrote. [5] 'He had collected round him over three hundred slave women, and the ill effects of this arrangement, and his indulgence in bhang and pombe, were plainly noticeable in his rapid decline into idiotcy.'

Nyangwe was made up by two different settlements on the banks of the Lualaba river. One was occupied by the wealthy Arabs, Swahilis and the leading members of the local population; the other was left to the poorer traders and the poor of the country.

On arrival Tippu Tip was led to the first settlement, and he was very much impressed with his countrymen's mode of life. He noticed the gardens planted with all kinds of Zanzibar fruit and vegetables, and the rice they grew in the surrounding swamps. 'Not for more than three years had we seen rice,' he remarks with delight. But most of all Tippu Tip wanted news of Zanzibar and the coast. He learnt that Sultan Majid had died in 1870 and that his brother and enemy, Barghash was now Sultan. They told him of the terrible cyclone which devastated the island in 1872 and caused enormous losses to plantation owners, and the arrival of an Englishman in Nyangwe who was now living in the house which was once occupied by Livingstone; but nobody

[5] V. Lovett Cameron, *Across Africa*, 1877.

mentioned that Sultan Barghash had signed the final treaty which forbade *all* his subjects to export slaves.

As usual Tippu Tip was fascinated by the idea of another white traveller, and he soon met Cameron. The latter says that Tippu Tip went to him, and Tippu Tip says Cameron looked for him and asked for his help. Whoever paid his respect first, Tippu Tip invited Cameron to travel to Kasongo with him, where he would give the explorer all the assistance he needed. According to Tippu Tip, the Nyangwe Arabs were furious at his sudden decision to leave for 'the sake of a white infidel'. Nevertheless, Cameron and his people joined Tippu Tip's caravan and left Nyangwe.

'He was a good-looking man, and the greatest dandy I had seen amongst the traders,' Cameron wrote of Tippu Tip. 'And notwithstanding his being perfectly black, he was a thorough Arab in his ideas and manners... Tipo-Tipo was accompanied by some of Russuna's (Rusuna) head-men, and the palaver concerning the attempted raid on that chief was quickly settled by the declaration of Tipo-Tipo that he would side with Russuna if he were again attacked. As his caravan, and those of five or six traders who recognised him as their head, could have brought more guns into the field than the Nyangwe people, and as the traders of Kwakasongo were also likely to have sided with Tipo-Tipo—he and his father being two of the richest and most influential of the travelling Zanzibar merchants—it was thought wise to promise to leave Russuna alone in future.'

Cameron was a very sick man. The 'fever' which had eventually killed Livingstone and so many other white men, including Cameron's last remaining English companion never left him as he walked day after day with Tippu Tip's caravan. He was often delirious and wandered about mistaking ant hills for his tent. His feet were blistered and his back covered with boils from infected mosquito bites, but he slit his boots and marched on.

Tippu Tip had to stop for a few days at his friend's village, to reassure Chief Rusuna that he need no longer worry about attacks from Nyangwe. They passed through fertile lands, 'with many fine trees, mpafu, gum-copal, African oak, teak, and others,' Cameron wrote. 'In one place there was a large grove of nutmeg-trees, and for forty or fifty yards the ground was literally covered with nutmegs.... We camped about two miles from Russuna's village, yet he, together with his brother and half a dozen wives, came to stay with us during our two days' halt. He visited me very often, bringing a different wife each time. They were the handsomest women I had seen in Africa, and in addition to their kilts of grass cloth [6] wore scarves of the same material across their breasts.... On the second day all fear of me and bashfulness had vanished, and they came in a body to see me. I soon had them all sitting around me looking at pictures and other curiosities; and after a time they began to wax so much more familiar that they turned up the legs and sleeves of my sleeping suit, which I always wore in camp, to discover whether it was my face alone that was white. Indeed, they ultimately became so inquisitive that I began to fear they would undress me altogether; to avoid which I sent for some beads and cowries and gave them a scramble, and thus withdrew their attention from my personal peculiarities.... When Russuna came to see me he brought a large and handsomely carved stool, upon which he sat, while he used the lap of one of his wives, who was seated on the ground, as his footstool.... Whilst we remained here a sub-chief visited him in state and.... they had a palaver with Tipo-Tipo and the Nyangwe Arabs, and after swearing eternal friendship the caravan was free to proceed to Tipo-Tipo's camp.... Russuna's private village, inhabited only by himself and his wives, we passed on the road. It consisted of about forty comfortable square huts in two rows, with a large one in the centre for himself. Each hut contained about four wives, and Russuna's mother had the pleasant task of keeping them all in order.'

Ten days later they reached Tippu Tip's camp and Kasongo's domain.

'Tipo-Tipo's camp was well arranged, and situated on a slight eminence; but not being a really permanent settlement, no large houses had been built, although Tipo-Tipo and the other traders had good huts. They provided me with a very comfortable one having two small apartments and a bath-room, besides sheds for my servants and cooking arrangements.

'Before making preparations for crossing the Lomami we had to receive a visit from Kasongo, the chief of the district, which took place two days after our arrival. At eight o'clock on that morning Tipo-Tipo, myself, and every leading man of his and Nyangwe parties, arrayed ourselves in our best—although I confess mine was not much of a turn-out—and assembled in an

[6] Viramba.

69

open shed, which was the general meeting place of the settlement during the day and often far into the night.

'An individual authorised by the chief to do duty as master of ceremonies then arrived, carrying a long carved walking-stick as a badge of office, his advent being the signal for all porters and slaves in camp and people from surrounding villages to crowd round to witness the spectacle. The M.C. drove the anxious sightseers back and formed a space near the reception room—as the hut may be termed—and then different sub-chiefs arrived, each followed by spearmen and shield bearers varying in number according to rank, a few of the more important being followed also by drummers.

'Each new-comer was brought to the entrance, where the Arabs and myself had taken our seats, and his name and rank proclaimed by the master of ceremonies, who further informed him of the position he was to occupy in order to be ready to welcome Kasongo.

'After some time spent in this manner, much drumming and shouting heralded the approach of the great man himself. First in the procession were half a dozen drummers, then thirty or forty spearmen, followed by six women carrying shields, and next Kasongo, accompanied by his brothers, eldest son, two of his daughters, and a few officials, the rear being brought up by spearmen, drummers, and marimba-players. On his reaching the entrance to the hut a ring was formed, and Kasongo—dressed in a jacket and kilt of red and yellow woollen cloth trimmed with long-haired monkey skins, [7] and with a greasy handkerchief tied round his head—performed a jigging dance with his two daughters.

'The Terpsichorean performance being concluded in about a quarter of an hour, he then entered the hut, and we had a long conversation.'

Kasongo showed great interest in Cameron's journey and promised his assistance.

'When Kasongo had taken his departure, which was conducted with much the same ceremony as that observed on arrival, I asked Tipo-Tipo to lend me a few men, and detailed an equal number of my own to accompany Kasongo's people to the Lomami.

'Two days after Kasongo's visit I returned his call, and found

[7] The outfit was a gift from Tippu Tip.

70

him sitting on an open grassy space in the middle of his village, which was composed of good-sized comfortable huts. He was dressed only in native grass-cloth, but looked far cleaner and more respectable than when tricked out in his tawdry finery.'

During Cameron's stay in Tippu Tip's camp, people had arrived from Urua with the news that Portuguese slavers were trading in their country. To support their story they showed Tippu Tip a Portuguese military coat one of the traders had given them. Cameron was anxious to go on with his explorations, but despite Kasongo's intervention, the neighbouring chief would not allow 'people carrying guns' through his territory. Cameron therefore abandoned the idea of going to the Lomami river, and instead decided to try and join the Portuguese party. Kasongo and Tippu Tip gave him guides and an escort and saw him off on the road to Urua.

'Besides these,' Cameron wrote, 'Tipo-Tipo also sent one of his leading men to journey ten days with me on the road.

'The only drawback I experienced to the comfort of Tipo-Tipo's camp was the number of slaves in chains who met my eyes at every turn; but, except being deprived of their freedom and confined in order to prevent their running away, they had a tolerable easy life, and were well fed.

'Tipo-Tipo and many Arab traders asserted that they would be glad to find other means of transport for their goods instead of trusting to slaves; but not regarding slave-dealing as a sin in the abstract, they availed themselves of the means at their disposal.'

One month later Cameron met the Portuguese half-castes and with them he reached Benguela on the West coast of Africa in November 1875. He was more dead than alive when he arrived but he was the first European to have crossed the entire African continent.

The Portuguese half-castes were not ideal companions, according to Cameron. They were the most cruel slavers he had ever met, but like Livingstone he was a sick man, and he could not afford to refuse their help.

Tippu Tip waited for a further three months at his camp for news of Cameron, and when none came he decided to move on to Kasongo, a district on the Lualaba River and nothing to do with Chief Kasongo Rushie. It was situated about thirty miles south of Nyangwe in Manyema, where he had heard one of his cousins had established a camp. He was tired of inactivity and he wanted to find new markets.

Chief Kasongo Rushie was greatly upset when he heard the news. He had become accustomed to a peaceful life in semi-retirement, and the prospect of losing his protector did not please him. Tippu Tip soon reassured him. He had arranged for one of his aides to stay behind with one hundred armed Wanyamwezi to carry on trading and protecting Kasongo's rich territory.

He ordered the ivory, the slaves, the porters and the guards assembled and marched off towards Nyangwe where the Arabs in that settlement invited him to stay and join forces with them. They told him he was crazy to go on to Kasongo where the people were rebellious and poor. Tippu Tip was too independent to join forces with anybody and he assured them that he would soon put things right when he arrived at his new destination.

The chiefs whose territories he crossed also invited him to stay and warned about the unrest and the famine at Kasongo. 'Don't worry,' Tippu Tip assured them in turn. 'When I get there it will all be in the hands of God.'

CHAPTER NINE

Henry Morton Stanley

Tippu Tip's cousin, Muhammed bin Said el Murjebi, was known as Bwana Nzige, or The Locust, because wherever his caravans passed, they left the country completely bare. Kasongo, where he had settled, was no exception. As soon as he crossed the frontier Tippu Tip realised that the reports had not been exaggerated. Kasongo was a miserable country.

Bwana Nzige was delighted to welcome his rich and powerful cousin. 'I am tired of this terrible country, Hamed,' he said. [1] 'When I first came here the people seemed co-operative and hard working, but they are not. They are a lot of lazy thieves like all the washenzi. Wherever I go, I have to move with a strong escort or they would cut my throat sooner than hand over a piece of ivory.'

'Perhaps you haven't treated them right,' Tippu Tip replied.

'Well, I have tried. Now you can try. As far as I am concerned you can take over completely. I will do whatever you think best.'

Tippu Tip did just that. He hadn't been at Kasongo for more than two days when two hundred of his slaves who were cutting wood in the vicinity of his camp, were stolen.

'Stolen? Nobody steals from me,' he shouted at the Arab in charge of the camp guards. 'You mean they ran away.'

'No, they didn't, Sultan. They were stolen.'

That was enough. He needed no further encouragement to organise one of his famous punitive missions. 'I decided on war,' he said to Brode many years later, reminiscing about Kasongo. 'And three months later they submitted and all remained smooth. Even women could travel safely through the country after I had been there a few months. I made sure that the ivory was sold

[1] Murjebi Family Papers.

to nobody else but us and I made the chiefs send their slaves to cultivate the fields. We grew rice and all kinds of produce and within no time at all people came from as far away as Nyangwe to buy from us.'

He had once again proved that he was more than just a trader bent on destruction for the mere sake of a few slaves and elephant tusks. Unlike other Arabs he did much more than exploit the country. After the initial fight and assertion of authority, he also gave the people protection from raiding neighbours and a degree of peace and prosperity. For this small service they had to pay, of course. Ivory and slaves were all that Tippu Tip demanded.

Once again life became very comfortable and profitable, so much so that when envoys came from Tabora with letters from his father and brother asking him to come back, he sent messages and presents to Tabora, but he didn't move. Instead he offered the Tabora envoys parcels of land to administer. Ivory was pouring in and Tippu Tip could not bear to leave such a rich market; but his father and his brother Muhammed were not going to resign themselves to being ignored. They had lost all contact with Tippu Tip for more than eight years, and having found him again, they kept sending messages.

Muhammed had waited for years in Samu's Itawa to hear from his brother, but when no word came, he had packed all the ivory and gone to Tabora. Now he wrote that he had sent the ivory to Taria Topan in Zanzibar, and he needed Tippu Tip's advice and help on many other questions. Finally Tippu Tip decided to leave, but not before going back to Utetera to chase away the Portuguese traders who were poaching in his territory, and not before taking delivery of a little more ivory his deputies had collected.

All this took months of course. It was October 1876 and the best equipped caravan Tippu Tip had ever seen marched into his territory. Henry Morton Stanley was on his second expedition and determined to complete the work started by Burton, Speke and Livingstone.

Stanley was born in Wales in 1841 of very poor parents. His name was then James Rowland, but being an ambitious young lad, he soon changed the course his life would have taken had he remained in Wales. He enlisted as cabin-boy and once his ship had reached New Orleans, he decided things looked better in America and he stayed behind. A kind old gentleman adopted him and gave him his name, Morton Stanley. He fought in the Civil War and worked at many things, but eventually he became a newspaper correspondent for the *New York Herald*. For that newspaper he had travelled to Europe, Russia, Turkey, Asia Minor, India and Abyssinia. Then came his great opportunity. The *New York Herald* sent him on the assignment which made him the most famous reporter in the world. 'Find Livingstone', the assignment said.

On the way he covered the opening of the Suez Canal in 1869 and his reports were published in the world press, but once he reached Zanzibar to organise 'the Livingstone relief expedition', not another word was published. Secrecy was all important. Such a scoop was not to be shared with any other publicity-seeking party. Stanley reached Livingstone at Ujiji in November 1871. He found the missionary explorer sick and destitute and living on charity from the Arabs. On Stanley's lavish supplies, Livingstone soon regained enough strength to accompany the American journalist on the exploration of Lake Tanganyika. They parted at Tabora, Livingstone to go back inland and to death, and Stanley back to the civilised world and fame. He had established himself as one of the great explorers and as such he was soon asked to undertake another expedition sponsored by the *New York Herald* and the *Daily Telegraph*.

He had no trouble recruiting suitable men for this difficult assignment. Out of twelve hundred applicants he chose Frederick Barker and the brothers Francis and Edward Pocock. In two weeks he purchased boats, guns, ammunition, tents, saddles, medical supplies and provisions, and by September 1874 he was back in Zanzibar hiring three hundred porters and buying beads, wire, cloth and all the other goods needed for barter along the route. Eight tons of supplies. As once before, he was assisted in his purchases by the richest merchant in Zanzibar, Tippu Tip's banker, Taria Topan who was 'singularly honest and just', Stanley declared.

Starting from Bagamoyo, he reached the Victoria Nyanza in February 1875, and in January 1876 he visited Mtesa, King of Uganda, who gave him two thousand spearmen. With them added to his large caravan he marched on to Lake Albert, then turned back towards Lake Tanganyika and on to Nyangwe and the meeting with Tippu Tip. These discoveries might have been enough for a lesser man, but Stanley was determined to solve the riddle of the Congo River and for this purpose he asked Tippu Tip's assistance. 'There was no person in Nyangwe whose evidence was more valuable than Tippu-Tib's,' he wrote.[2]

They first met on the Lualaba River in October 1876 and the impression Stanley recorded of Tippu Tip, was very flattering.[3] In the course of their long and not always friendly association, Stanley's opinion of Tippu Tip as an 'Arab gentleman' changed considerably, and at the end of their relationship many years later, Tippu Tip's opinion of Stanley as a 'European gentleman', did not rate very high either.

For the time being, however, the Arab gentleman and the explorer were delighted with each other.

From Tippu Tip Stanley found out that both Livingstone and Cameron had been frustrated in their efforts to follow the Lualaba by the lack of canoes and because 'Cameron's men decidedly opposed following the river, as no one knew whither it went.'[2] The river was not the only obstacle, 'the great wall of trees' north of Nyangwe had resisted all attempts of penetration by the Arabs and the local tribes. The few caravans which travelled north had returned decimated and with horrifying stories of murderous pigmies, boa-constrictors, gorillas and never-ending forests.

'If you wasungu[4] wish to throw away your lives, it is no reason we Arabs should,' Tippu Tip said to Stanley[5] when the explorer proposed that the Arab and some of his men should accompany him part of the way. 'We travel little by little to get ivory and slaves, and are years about it.... but you white men only look for rivers and lakes and mountains, and you spend your lives for no reason, and to no purpose. Look at that old man who died in Bisa![6] What did he seek year after year, until he became so old that he could not travel? He had no money, for he never gave any of us anything, he bought no ivory or slaves, yet he travelled farther than any of us, and for what?'

'I know I have no right to expect you to risk your life for me,' Stanley replied. 'I only wish you to accompany me sixty days' journey, then leave me to myself.... You know the Wang-

[2] Henry Morton Stanley's *Through the Dark Continent*.
[3] See page ix.
[4] Wasungu=White men.
[5] All quotations in this chapter from Stanley's *Through the Dark Continent*.
[6] Livingstone.

wana are easily swayed by fear, but if they hear that Tippu-Tib
has joined me, and is about to accompany me, every man will
have a lion's courage.'

Tippu Tip promised he would think about it and after a night's
sleep he would give his answer. The next evening he went to the
house he had given Stanley, together with his cousin Bwana
Nzige.

'After the usual courteous and ceremonious greetings,' Stanley
wrote, 'I was requested to state my intentions.

'I would like to go down the river in canoes until I reach the
place where the river turns for good either to the west or to the
east,' he said.

'How many days' journey on land would that be?' Tippu Tip
asked.

'I don't know. Do you?'

'No; indeed, I was never in that direction; but I have a man
here who has reached furthest of all.'

A young Arab was then called in. Yes, he knew all about
the river, he said. And in which direction does it flow? Stanley
wanted to know. It flows north. And then? It flows north! And
then? Still north.

'Come my friend, speak,' Stanley said. 'Whither does it flow
after reaching the north?'

'Why master,' replied he, with a bland smile of wonder at
my apparent lack of ready comprehension, 'don't I tell you it
flows north, and north, and north, and there is no end to it? I
think it reaches the salt sea, at least some of my friends say so.'

The young Arab then went on to describe the time when he
was a member of a strong caravan pursuing tales of the richest
ivory country they had ever seen. 'The dwarfs were very curious
to know what we wanted with it,' the young man said to Stanley.
They only ate the elephant meat and threw away the tusks, he
explained. 'We reached Uregga, a forest land ... where there is
nothing but woods, and woods, and woods, for days, and weeks,
and months. There was no end to the woods. The people lived
surrounded by woods ... we fought day after day. They were fearful fellows and desperate. We lost men every day. Every man
of ours that was killed was eaten. They were hiding behind such
thick bushes that we could not see them, and their arrows were
poisoned....' The caravan collected more ivory than they could
carry, but the pigmies fought them every inch of the way and

77

they were running short of powder, water and food. 'At last we ran away, throwing down everything except our guns and swords ... but nearly all were so weakened by hunger and want of water that they burst their hearts running, and died. Others lying down to rest found the little devils close to them when too late, and were killed. Master, out of that great number of people that left Nyangwe, Arabs, Wangwana, and our slaves, only thirty returned alive, and I am one of them.'

'Did you see anything else very wonderful on your journey?' Stanley asked to show the Arabs he had not been taken in by the story. Tippu Tip looked at him but said nothing.

'Oh yes!' The young Arab replied. 'There are monstrous large boa-constrictors in the forest of Uregga, suspended by their tails to the branches, waiting for the passer-by or for a stray antelope. The ants in that forest are not to be despised. You cannot travel without your body being covered with them, they sting you like wasps. The leopards are so numerous that you cannot go very far without seeing one. The sokes (gorillas) are in the woods, and woe befall the man or woman met alone by them; for they run up to you and seize your hands, and bite the fingers off one by one, and as fast as they bite one off, they spit it out.'

Stanley thanked the Arab for the information and then turned to Tippu Tip. 'What did you think of all that?' he asked.

'Well, I have heard it all before,' Tippu Tip replied. He didn't add that each time he had heard the story, the details were improved upon, and that despite the reports and his conviction that the journey would not be an easy one, he had already decided to travel with Stanley. They signed an agreement for Tippu Tip to supply porters and an escort for a distance of sixty camps and Tippu Tip showed Stanley his stores of ivory to impress upon the white man that he had no need to earn any more money, he was only doing Stanley a kindness. Stanley in turn showed off his guns, [7] and finally they shook hands.

[7] See page x.

CHAPTER TEN

Looking for the Congo River with Stanley

It was quite true that Tippu Tip didn't need the money Stanley had promised him for the three months' journey, but neither was it true that he accepted to undertake such a trip out of sheer kindness. Tippu Tip was always anxious to extend his 'sphere of influence', and he couldn't forgo the opportunity of pushing north of Nyangwe supported by such a well equipped caravan as Stanley's. He laughed at the Nyangwe Arabs who told him he was crazy to follow an unbeliever who didn't know where he was going.

'Do you think you will become a European after all these trips with white men, Hamed?' they teased him.[1]

'And do you think you will become a woman after all your trips to the harem?' he laughed back at them. 'You all stay at home and look after the harem like eunuchs. I'm a man and a man travels where fortune takes him. Don't worry about me. I know where I'm going.'

A dozen Arabs, each attended by five or six female slaves and forty male slaves armed with 'flintlocks', accompanied Tippu Tip. These were his dependants, Stanley says,[2] 'who dip their hands in the same porridge and meat dish'. And, of course, part of Tippu Tip's harem went along to attend to his comforts. Stanley described them as 'twenty handsome women'. There were people from the coast, Wangwana from Zanzibar, porters from Unyamwezi, slaves from Utetera, Manyema and all the other regions

[1] Murjebi Family Papers.

[2] All quotes in this chapter are from Stanley's *Through the Dark Continent*.

which paid tribute to Tippu Tip. All were armed with spears or guns. There were also about fifty young slaves, ranging from ten to eighteen years of age, who had been trained by Tippu Tip as gun-bearers, servants, scouts, cooks, carpenters, builders and blacksmiths. 'Such young fellows are useful to him,' Stanley wrote. 'They are more trustworthy than adults, because they look up to him as their father, and know that if they left him they would inevitably be captured by a less humane man.'

The huge caravan left Nyangwe on the 5th of November, 1876, and by the 6th they approached 'the dreaded black and chill forest called Mitamba, bidding farewell to sunshine and brightness. Every leaf seemed weeping,' Stanley noted. 'Down the boles and branches, creepers and vegetable cords, the moisture trickled and fell on us. Overhead the wide spreading branches, in many interlaced strata, each branch heavy with broad thick leaves, absolutely shut out the daylight. We marched in a feeble solemn twilight. The path soon became a stiff clayey paste, and every step we splashed water ...' It was hard going, but hardest of all it was for the porters who carried the *Lady Alice*, the forty foot long steel and cedar boat, which had been dismantled into sections for easier carriage. Even so, the sections were too large for the narrow animal paths, and every day the whole caravan lost hours waiting for the boat-carriers to catch up. At night the huge caravan struggled into the temporary camps, but the boat-carriers always arrived much later than anybody else, and sometimes they didn't arrive at all. 'The boat sections—dreadful burdens,' Stanley says, 'had to be driven like blunted ploughs through the depths of foliage. The men complained bitterly of fatigue ... and what we have experienced as yet is only a poor beginning to the weeks upon weeks which we shall have to endure. Such crawling, scrambling, tearing through the damp, dank jungles, and such height and depth of woods!'

Marching became harder every day. 'Our expedition is no longer the compact column which was my pride. It is utterly demoralised.' The porters slipped and fell, or their loads were caught in the vegetation. Tippu Tip organised a party to walk ahead of the boat carriers and cut a path through the thick vegetation, but it still took twenty four porters a whole day to cover six miles. Stanley and his only remaining English companion,[3]

[3] Frederick Barker and Edward Pocock died before Stanley met Tippu Tip.

Frank Pocock, in ten days had worn out all but their last pair of boots. In a situation of almost unsurmountable obstacles, the boots became one more unbearable problem. 'Even Tippu-Tib, whom I anxiously watched,' Stanley recorded, 'as on him I staked all my hopes and prospects, murmured.'

Tippu Tip did more than murmur. From the very beginning he had argued with his followers, but now after ten days of crawling through the stifling atmosphere of the 'pagan's forest', as they referred to the Uregga forest, he was losing control over his men, and this he could not allow. Together with his cousin and the other Arabs, on the evening of the 10th day, he went to Stanley's tent and announced his intention of 'dissolving their contract'. What Stanley had feared would happen—the end of his expedition—was now almost a certainty. Failure was a word he had left behind in Wales, and he wasn't about to let it catch up with him now.

He used every argument his very nimble mind could think of. Honour, reputation, danger, the anger of the Sultan and the British Consul in far away Zanzibar; nothing affected Tippu Tip's decision.

'It is no use having two tongues,' Tippu Tip answered. 'Look at it how you may, these sixty camps will take over a year, at the rate we are travelling, and it will take as much to return. I was never in this forest before, and I had no idea that there was such a place in the world; but the air is killing my people, it is insufferable. You will kill your own people if you go on. They are grumbling every day more and more. This country was not made for travel; it was made for vile pagans, monkeys, and wild beasts. I cannot go further.'

'For two hours I plied him with arguments,' Stanley says. 'And at last, when I was nearly exhausted, Tippu-Tib consented to accompany me twenty marches further.' Stanley could have argued for much longer and not convinced Tippu Tip, but two thousand six hundred dollars were mentioned during the argument, and Tippu Tip graciously consented to go on.

It was agreed to cut through to the Lualaba River as quickly as the men would march, and then sail down the river on Stanley's boat and the canoes they planned to buy from the local tribesmen. From the scanty information they had been able to collect at Nyangwe, Stanley calculated that the falls and cataracts had now been bypassed, and at least some of the caravan

81

could follow the river. Tippu Tip of course says that Stanley begged him not to leave him in the forest and completely lost his head. Again out of kindness (no mention of money), he talked the men into following the white man for a further twenty marches.

Nine days later, and only forty one miles north of Nyangwe, they sighted the river again, a confluent of the great Congo which Stanley named the *Livingstone*. The river was one thousand two hundred yards wide at that point, and whilst the men rested and Stanley sat with Tippu Tip on the grassy banks planning the next move down the uncharted waters, Frank Pocock and a few helpers set about reconstructing the *Lady Alice*.

Another 'wall of trees' faced them on the opposite bank, and little islands dotted the deep river. Through his binoculars the explorer could see hundreds of people by the river, and some of them were rowing their canoes towards them. He watched them approach and then through an interpreter he asked them to sell him canoes. The only answer was wild cries and shouts, which were promptly answered up and down the banks of the river. 'That is a war-cry,' Tippu Tip informed him as he loaded his gun. [4]

'Nonsense, don't be foolish. What cause is there for war?' Stanley replied.

'These people don't need a cause. They're wild beasts,' Tippu Tip assured him.

He had already warned Stanley about cataracts, cannibals and war-like tribes, but although during their march through the forest they had come across a few isolated villages which obviously indulged in cannibalism; Stanley still believed that this was very much the exception, rather than the rule. He was fascinated by the skulls which decorated the Waregga villages. The inhabitants assured him that they were chimpanzee skulls, but when he took some back to England, they were identified as human. The meat was very good the villagers assured him. He found the Waregga admirable in other ways too. They forged their own spears and knives, and made furniture. He had never seen Africans making 'settees out of cane, and backgammon trays', he says. All the more surprising as the Waregga were completely isolated and surrounded by the forest.

Despite his past experiences, Stanley still believed that he

[4] Murjebi Family Papers.

could 'reason' with the Africans. The canoe owners were obviously not interested in 'reason', and as they started throwing spears and shooting arrows, the only way to convince them of their 'peaceful intentions', was to fire at them, Tippu Tip says.

The *Lady Alice* was ready for launching, and by the time Stanley had finished his breakfast, which he took in the privacy of his tent, the boat was in the river.

With Tippu Tip, some of his Arabs and the boat crew, he crossed the river and approached the people on the left bank, the interpreter all the time shouting that all the white man wanted was canoes. He was a generous man and would give them many shells.

'The natives, gazing curiously at me, promised after a consultation, that if we made blood-brotherhood with them there should be no trouble,' Stanley says.

Frank Pocock was chosen for the brotherhood ceremony but somehow the 'natives became restless' and Tippu Tip's force had to rescue the long suffering Pocock.

A small camp was established on the left bank, and the river people had it explained to them that 'it would be far better that they should assist us in the ferriage, for which they might feel assured they would be well paid,' Stanley wrote. 'At the same time I tossed a small bag of beads to them. In a few minutes they consented, and six canoes, with two men in each, accompanied us to camp ... By night every soul associated with our Expedition was rejoicing by genial camp-fires in the village of the Wenya.'

Tippu Tip never mentioned the rejoicing by the camp fires, the only time he rejoiced was when the villagers fled and he captured large numbers of goats. Of the same deserted village, Stanley says, 'We had hoped to pass our first day in the Wenya land in kindly interchange of gifts ... but lo! when we searched in the morning for the aborigines they were gone!'

They were all gone. Up and down the river the villages were all deserted, but 'each village street had its two rows of bleached trophies of eaten humanity, with an attempt at a ghastly decoration similar to rockery.' However, the villagers had left their canoes, their goats and their crops behind. Stanley had instructed his people 'on penalty of fearful punishment', that nothing should be touched because he wanted to establish the 'right kind of trustworthy intercourse' with the local people.

As they floated down the river, the *Lady Alice* carrying thirty-six men, and the rest of the party travelling along the banks, they were preceded by the beating of drums and war-cries warning the villagers to hide in the forest as the strangers approached. Every night they camped on the river banks and waited for the land party to join them, but one night the land party, led by Tippu Tip on that occasion, didn't arrive at all. The next day Stanley, together with a few men, decided to row up-river again to look for the missing five hundred, but there was no sign of them, and by the time he returned to their camp, he found it surrounded by hundreds of screaming warriors and canoes. It seems that the villagers along the river had decided to get their evening meal, but Stanley's unexpected arrival made them change their mind, and they retreated.

It was not until the following day that the land party finally joined them, and a miserable sight they were. Weary, haggard, sick and low spirited, they had lost their way, wandered through the forest and been attacked.

The river widened and the islands became bigger. They kept in touch with the land party by drum signals and all the villages they passed were deserted. People ran for the forest as they approached and screamed warnings to the others that the raiders were coming. Livestock, food and canoes were abandoned, and at one point Stanley was 'forced' to appropriate six canoes, which were lashed together to form a floating hospital for the many victims of small-pox and dysentery.

Another problem suddenly and unpleasantly presented itself. A half mile of rapids. Stanley immediately ordered the hospital canoes and the *Lady Alice* to make for the shore, and with a small scouting party he proceeded to assess the situation. Another scouting party also left camp against his orders, and this was all the locals were waiting for. They attacked the second group, Stanley went to the rescue, and Tippu Tip chose that occasion to announce that he was leaving.

'I've had enough now,' he said. [5] 'Impenetrable forests, cannibals, small-pox, dysentery and now rapids, and you will never take my advice. It's time for me to turn back.'

Once more Stanley talked him into staying until the next morning, and by then Tippu Tip's mood seems to have improved. In fact, on that occasion Tippu Tip did feel sorry for the harassed explorer.

[5] Murjebi Family Papers.

TIPPU TIP

ZANZIBAR HARBOUR AND FLEET OF DHOWS

SLAVERS REVENGING THEIR LOSSES

LIVINGSTONE

SLAVES ABANDONED

STANLEY

SULTAN BARGHASH

SIR JOHN KIRK

STANLEY EMIN PASHA RELIEF EXPEDITION LEAVING MATADI

The *Lady Alice* was lifted out of the water and with dreadful difficulties, carried past the rapids, and the canoes were unfastened and left to drift down the ten foot drop. All was ready for the next day's sailing down the unpredictable river.

It was the first of December, almost one month since they had left Nyangwe, and the travelling by land and river was no easier than it had been on their first day through the forest. The river became more treacherous, and the villagers along the banks more daring. The black forest flanked the river on both sides and the land party, first commanded by Frank Pocock and then by Tippu Tip, travelled at the same pace as they had travelled through the forest. More and more people died of small-pox, dysentery, ulcers and pneumonia, and there were even a few cases of typhoid. The hospital canoes were full, and every day the dead were thrown overboard. Stanley and Frank Pocock did their best with their scant medical knowledge and limited medical supplies, but even Tippu Tip recognised their kindness when three of his women became victims of the small-pox and died.

Great crowds from the surrounding forests and islands met on neutral ground to barter the produce of their rich land. They bartered with their local enemies, but not with the slavers from Nyangwe. Word of the Arab slavers had been passed on from village to village, and when the drums beat, they either fled or attacked. The attacks were becoming more frequent and any attempt Stanley made to convince the river people that he was not a slaver on a raiding expedition, was received with a shower of poisoned arrows.

Great flotillas of large war canoes chased them down the river and bands of warriors ambushed the land party. On some occasions they landed at a deserted village and helped themselves to food and goats, but often the people came back at night and fighting started. The river people had no guns but they shot their poisoned arrows with deadly accuracy and the two white men were kept busy pulling out arrows and cauterizing the wounds. They took a few prisoners to obtain information of the river and the tribes ahead of them, but the reports were not encouraging. All the prisoners they released were amazed that Stanley and his men did not want to eat them.

'Sleep, under such circumstances, was out of the question,' Stanley wrote. 'Yet there were many weak, despairing souls whom even the fear of being eaten could not rouse to a sense of

85

manliness and the necessity for resistance.' To keep people awake when they were being surrounded and attacked after a hard day of walking or rowing, Stanley ordered buckets of cold water to be poured on each man as he keeled over through exhaustion. Most nights the only occupants of the camp were the forty men from the *Lady Alice* and the sick.

One evening after settling in camp, Stanley noticed dozens of war canoes converging on the opposite island. They were 'manned by such a dense mass of men that any number between five hundred and eight hundred would be within the mark,' he says. It was not long before the canoes drew up in battle formation and blowing their war horns attacked. Stanley only had forty men with him, the land party had not arrived yet.

'The battle had continued half an hour with a desperate energy, only qualified by our desperate state,' Stanley wrote. 'Ammunition we possessed in abundance, and we made use of it with deadly effect, yet what might have become of us is doubtful had not the advance-guard of Tippu-Tib and our land division arrived at this crucial juncture.'

After Tippu Tip's arrival the war canoes retired to the island to prepare themselves for the next day's assault. Stanley decided this had to be avoided at all cost. Together with Pocock and a handful of chosen men, he embarked on the *Lady Alice* and quietly rowed to the island. It was a misty and rainy night, and as they approached they could hear the warriors talking and laughing by the fires. They had tied their long canoes together with reeds and secured them to stakes on the muddy banks. Gliding quietly under the shadows of the trees, Stanley and his men cut the reeds and pushed the canoes into the fast flowing stream. They took twelve of them in tow and by five o'clock of the following morning, not one canoe was left to the confident warriors. The peace talks were not long in coming. Another blood-brotherhood ceremony took place, some of the canoes were returned and some bought and the warriors, assured of the expedition's peaceful intentions, allowed them to leave.

It was the 22nd of December and Tippu Tip firmly announced his intention of returning to Nyangwe. This time Stanley did not try to dissuade him. He now had enough boats to carry his hundred and forty nine men, women and children, and although Tippu Tip still owed him eight marches, Stanley decided to be generous and let him go.

According to Tippu Tip most of Stanley's men refused to follow Stanley any further when they heard that the Arabs and their followers were turning back, but in his usual helpful manner, he talked them into following the white men down to the sea. He would make sure that Stanley would remunerate them handsomely.

The Arab and the explorer were obviously jealous of the influence each had on the caravan. Stanley writes of Tippu Tip's undisciplined people, and his own generosity in rewarding them for their services. 'I gave Tippu-Tib a draft for 2,600 dollars,' he says. 'One riding ass, one trunk, one gold chain, thirty doti of fine cloth, one hundred and fifty pounds of beads, sixteen thousand three hundred shells, one revolver, two hundred rounds of ammunition and fifty pounds of brass wire.' To each Arab and their men he gave cloth suitable to their rank, and according to him they were all satisfied.

'Not so,' Tippu Tip says.[6] 'I had to force Stanley to reward my people, and in his usual lying manner he promised me much wealth and a watch worth a thousand dollars, surrounded with diamonds, and a countless sum of money.'

Such accusations and recriminations came later, at the time both parties were busy reorganising and restocking, one for the return journey, and the other for the continuation of his explorations.

Finally all was ready. The food had been assembled, the small canoes tied in pairs so they wouldn't capsize, and as far as the only two Christians were concerned, all that remained to do was celebrate the birth of their Redeemer.

Tippu Tip and his followers were delighted with the Christmas celebrations. Stanley had organised a great feast of meat and rice for the whole caravan, and even palm-wine was served. Later there were boat races, but the great event of the day was the race between Tippu Tip and Frank Pocock.

'The Arab prepared himself with unusual determination,' Stanley says, 'to compete for the prize, a richly chased silver goblet and cup. Though Frank exerted himself to the utmost, the sinews of the muscular Arab carried him to the front of the finish by fifteen yards.'

Even the women were induced to race, and 'their presence on

[6] Murjebi Family Papers.

the racecourse convulsed the hundreds assembled to witness the unusual scene.'

Not to be outdone in generosity, the next day Tippu Tip returned the invitation and treated Stanley's party to a rich banquet of roasted sheep, rice and palm-wine.

On the 27th of December they parted company, Stanley to follow the river he believed to be the Congo, and Tippu Tip overland to Nyangwe and more remunerative trading.

In his book *Through the Dark Continent*, Stanley often indulges in poetic phrases, and the description of the parting with Tippu Tip is no exception. 'Ranged along the bank in picturesque costume the sons of Unyamwezi sang their last song,' he wrote. 'We waved our hands to them. Our hearts were so full of grief that we could not speak. Steadily the brown flood bore us by, and fainter and fainter came the notes down the water, till finally they died away, leaving us all alone in our loneliness.' A little too dramatic for modern ears perhaps, but one can understand Stanley's feelings at the prospect of facing the unknown with a small band of men and only Frank Pocock to share his fears. Falls, cataracts, sickness, starvation and continual attacks were all in front of them, and before reaching the sea in August 1877, his last remaining friend, Frank Pocock, was to die swallowed by the swirling waters of the Congo.

CHAPTER ELEVEN

Missionaries and Mirambo

As far as Tippu Tip was concerned, the parting with Stanley was not a difficult one. In fact, he was relieved to be rid of such a demanding employer. Besides, he didn't like to be told what to do, nor did he like to take second place to any man in any venture.

He had promised Stanley he would wait for a month to make sure he got through the first part of the journey; but of course, he didn't waste time sitting on the banks of the river. He sent scouting parties into the forest and decided on what course to take on his way back to Nyangwe. The district between the Lualaba and the Lomami was reported to be rich in ivory, and after a month he moved off towards that area.

He was delighted to leave the river and the forest behind him, to go on trading and dealing with people as he always had, without another man telling him what to do.

The people of the Lomami had no idea that ivory was a valuable commodity. They used the tusks to fence their villages and for household utensils, or merely threw them away as they only killed elephants for the meat.

Tippu Tip was not the man to inform them of the real value of their fences and pestles. For three dollars worth of beads he bought ten thousand dollars' worth of ivory, and all this in peace and harmony—but not for very long.

Other tribes, although like their neighbours they had no use for ivory, were not interested in trading with the Arabs, and there was 'fighting every day', Tippu Tip says. Which means that he had to adopt his old methods. The poisoned arrows were a nuisance but they had learnt from Stanley how to cauterize the wounds immediately, and the losses to his caravan were negligible.

He reached Nyangwe a richer man than when he had left, and

although the Arabs of that settlement welcomed him back and invited him to stay a while, he was anxious to reach his own territory of Kasongo, and the next day he sailed down the Lualaba.

At Kasongo all was ready for his return. As instructed before his departure, the agents had come from every district as far as Urua and Utetera to bring their stocks of ivory. This pleased Tippu Tip, and he felt somewhat compensated for the time wasted with Stanley.

For the next two years he travelled and traded in his vast territories, appointing more deputies to take care of his business and introducing them to the chiefs. To his cousin Muhammed bin Said, The Locust, he assigned Kasongo Rushie's region and Bwana Nzige was quite satisfied to be left there for good as he found the people peaceful, the land fertile and the women very pleasing, he said. On the other hand, the old chief said: 'Nobody can take your place. I shall wait to die until you return,' which Tippu Tip found very touching.

His relations and lieutenants were taking good care of his dominions, and Tippu Tip decided it was time to start moving the enormous stocks of ivory towards Tabora and the coast. Sultan Barghash, whom he had never met, had sent him a 'repeating gun' and other gifts with a request that the trader should come back to Zanzibar to settle his affairs. His banker, Taria Topan had sent him a shot-gun and clothes, and as the two year credit had expired many years before, would Tippu Tip consider returning to Zanzibar, the banker asked. Stanley had gone back to Europe via Zanzibar, and he had said 'very nice things' about Tippu Tip, the banker wrote. He added that he was pleased to tell him that the explorer had paid three thousand dollars into Tippu Tip's account, and had left Tippu Tip a photo of himself.

'That's what he left me,' Tippu Tip exploded. [1] 'After all he promised. A photograph. That's all he left. Can a man eat photographs?'

As Stanley had given him a draft for two thousand six hundred dollars when they parted, three thousand to his banker, and a number of gifts, he must have felt that he had been very generous considering Tippu Tip had broken his contract before the agreed time had expired.

There was so much ivory to transport that the two thousand

[1] Murjebi Family Papers.

porters and one thousand guards had to travel many times back and forth to Mtoa on Lake Tanganyika before all the ivory was ready for shipping across the lake to Ujiji.

Tippu Tip had not been to Ujiji for over twenty years. The last time he had gone it was with his father on their second expedition, and twenty years had brought many changes to the lake. In 1878 the London Missionary Society had sent an expedition to Ujiji and the first mission station was established under Edward Hore. Not long after, in 1879, the French Catholic White Fathers had set up a mission a few miles south of Ujiji and Hore predicted that the Catholics would not 'hinder us much as they are quite unfit and unprovided for this work'. Whatever Hore thought of the opposition, the White Fathers remained. The London Missionary Society in the meantime opened another mission at Mtua, on the west side of the lake, and there Tippu Tip met Griffiths, the head of the new mission.

A third European organisation had settled on Lake Tanganyika. The African International Association founded by Leopold II of Belgium had established a station on the Lake as a 'philanthropic effort to civilise the tribes to the west of the Tanganyika,' the Association's charter stated.

The newcomers' primary undertaking was the abolition of slavery, but in 1881 the head of the Missionary Society at Mtua, Mr. Griffiths, welcomed the greatest slaver of them all. Tippu Tip says that he made friends with the European missionary and the doctor and that they treated him with 'great respect'.

Tippu Tip's greatest worry was now Mirambo. The warrior chief referred to, by European travellers, as the Napoleon of Africa.

Mirambo's grandfather had been appointed chief of Ugoa, a small area within the large Unyamwezi district, assisted by Tippu Tip's grandfather, but within a few years of his becoming chief, Mirambo terrorised and occupied a huge stretch of land which extended from south of Lake Victoria to Lake Tanganyika. Whilst Tippu Tip dominated the countries west of Lake Tanganyika, Mirambo and his army of Ruga-Ruga[2] controlled all the routes

[2] Ruga-Ruga has sometimes been translated as 'bandit' and sometimes as 'mercenary'. The Ruga-Ruga army was composed of runaway slaves, deserting porters, guards and elephant hunters; but mostly they were Ngoni warriors, a group of Zulu raiders who had pushed their way as far as Unyamwezi and settled there. They wore red cloaks, feather head-dress, and ivory and copper ornaments.

east of the lake as far as Tabora. His capital and headquarters was north of Tabora and he named the place Urambo. He demanded and obtained more hongo than any chief had ever extracted from caravans travelling through his territory, and the Arabs were terrified of him. During Stanley's visit to Tabora, the Arabs, supported by Baluchi soldiers from Zanzibar, declared war on Mirambo with devastating consequences for the Arabs.

By 1881, when Tippu Tip's enormous caravan was preparing to cross the lake, Mirambo had complete control of the roads leading from Tabora north to Buganda and west to Ujiji.

The Rev. Thomson, who headed the first group sent out by the London Missionary Society in 1878, was very impressed by Mirambo. Thomson noted that he was about forty years old, well built and very active. He also says that Mirambo was six foot ten, or eleven inches tall, and that he had twenty five wives and five children. The Reverend's figures are somewhat puzzling. However, Mirambo seems to have taken a liking to white missionaries, and in 1879 he allowed Dr. Southon, also of the L.M.S. to settle in Urambo.

Dr. Southon describes Urambo as 'a large square enclosure the sides of which are composed of a substantially built wall against which houses are built all round. It is nearly half a mile square and encloses nearly two square miles of ground. In the space thus enclosed about two hundred round huts—well built and some of them fifty feet in diameter—give habitation to about 10,000 habitants; quite another 5,000 live in the houses built against the wall. The industrious agriculturalists and enterprising wapagazi (porters) live at a distance from the capital; the former supplying food for the army, the latter carrying the plunder to Zanzibar and returning with guns, powder and the like.'

Mirambo's success was partly due to his electrifying personality,[3] and partly to his well armed and trained Ruga-Ruga warriors. But most of all, the success of Mirambo's army, as of the Arabs before him, was due to his acquiring guns, either through raids on passing caravans, or merely bartering for them with slaves and cattle which he captured from his weaker neighbours.

Mirambo hated all Arabs, and in particular the Tabora Arabs with whom he fought innumerable battles. On many occasions

[3] Both Cameron and Stanley, who met him, recorded this fact.

he sent messengers to Consul Kirk in Zanzibar asking him to 'do something about the Arabs of Tabora'. He wanted the head of that community removed and he wanted to be recognised as the supreme chief of all Unyamwezi with the Arabs paying tribute to *him*. Sultan Barghash was more than prepared to come to terms with the great Mirambo. All the Sultan wanted was a peaceful continuation of trade between the coast and the lake, and Mirambo was disrupting that trade. The Tabora Arabs, with their continual squabbles among themselves and ineffectual wars on Mirambo were no help to the Sultan of Zanzibar, and the Sultan was not strong enough to defeat Mirambo. There was only one thing to do, and Consul Kirk advised Barghash to do it. Agree to Mirambo's terms and let him be responsible for the peaceful continuation of trade.

Unfortunately for Mirambo, when Kirk and Barghash were about to make an offer, his followers attacked a Church Missionary Society caravan killing 150 porters and a missionary by the name of Penrose. They later killed every member of a Belgian scientific expedition, headed by an Englishman named Carter. On both occasions Mirambo claimed that he knew nothing of these attacks and was therefore not responsible. By disclaiming responsibility for the actions of his followers, he of course proved that he was not the right man to keep the peace in Unyamwezi.

This was the man Tippu Tip had to defeat or come to terms with before he could transport his amassed wealth to Tabora.

Despite Kirk's efforts to curb the sale of guns and powder on the mainland, Sultan Barghash could not or would not control the ever increasing traffic of firearms, therefore more and more chiefs turned into 'war lords' and followed Mirambo's example. None of them achieved his greatness but even so, no caravan was safe travelling between Ujiji and Tabora.

Tippu Tip decided it would be most unwise to travel through such country with two thousand tusks. In Ujiji he was a guest of Muhammed bin Khalfan, known as Rumaliza, and one of the most powerful traders there. In later years Tippu Tip and Rumaliza were to become partners and then bitter enemies, but for the time being Rumaliza showed great pleasure and pride in welcoming as famous a man as Tippu Tip.

With Rumaliza's assistance Tippu Tip arranged to store most of his ivory in Ujiji and proceed to Tabora with the smaller tusks and a strong escort, first of all to test the safety of the road and then to obtain ammunition, provisions and more porters from his father.

No sooner had he left Ujiji than two of his porters were killed. The next morning a whole crowd of Ruanda tribesmen attacked the caravan 'for no reason', Tippu Tip says. He had decided to reach Tabora as quickly and as peacefully as possible, but it was against his nature to forgive such an insult and he immediately retaliated. Within half an hour the attackers had left twenty seven dead on the field and Tippu Tip's escort chased the rest back to their villages. Fifteen villages were burnt in one day.

The Ruanda district [4] was rich in sugar-cane, maize, rice and beans, and Tippu Tip's men gladly helped themselves.

During the month they stayed in Ruanda, his eighteen years old son, Sef arrived with a group of Arab traders. A wonderful surprise for Tippu Tip who had left him in Zanzibar as a very small boy, but at first he was angry that Sef had been allowed to travel through such dangerous country.

'I am not a child anymore, father,' Sef assured him. [5] 'I am as ready to fight as any of your followers here and when I heard you were going back to Tabora, I couldn't just stay at home with the women.'

Tippu Tip was delighted. It didn't seem so long ago that he had said much about the same words to his own father.

'You will be a great help to me, my son,' he said hugging him.

With Sef he started again for Tabora travelling through Uvinza country. Chief Kasanura of Uvinza was one of the strongest war lords on the Ujiji-Tabora route, and he harassed Tippu Tip's caravan, demanding large quantities of hongo, stealing 150 slaves and killing a number of porters. Tippu Tip was all for starting another punitive campaign, but he was advised against it by an Arab who had joined the caravan and lost everything at Kasanura's hands. This time he marched on deciding to postpone the pleasure of retaliation.

His father and his brother were waiting for them at Ituru, and the celebrations for his return went on for two weeks. Tabora, like Ujiji, had changed and some of the changes had been brought by the White Fathers who had recently opened a mission there. Wissman, the German explorer, was very much impressed by the

[4] The Ruanda district, east of Ujiji and not to be confused with the important Hima Kingdom in the north.
[5] Murjebi Family Papers.

94

Catholic missionaries. 'They have already left their mark on the country around,' he wrote. [6] 'In contradistinction to the Evangelical missions, which chiefly devoted themselves to doctrinal efforts, the Catholics attached more importance to practical training in civilisation. With but narrow means at their disposal, they had installed themselves admirably. Gardening, agriculture, and cattle-breeding flourished under their guidance.'

The Tabora Arabs were greatly concerned at the success of the Christian missionaries, but Tippu Tip considered the newly established station of the Belgian African International Association, far more dangerous to Arab interests. He immediately sent messages of loyalty to Sultan Barghash, and a request for gun powder.

The Sultan replied by special courier. 'I have instructed Taria Topan to supply you with 2,000 pounds of gun powder. Please accept it. No payment is necessary.' Having lost faith in Mirambo, the Sultan's last remaining hope for the trade routes, was now Tippu Tip, and to him he was prepared to give all he asked for.

Other messengers arrived in Tabora whilst Tippu Tip was restocking the caravan for the return trip to Ujiji to collect the rest of the ivory. Mirambo sent a message to say that he had no quarrel with the great Tippu Tip. He was welcome to travel through his country unmolested. He still hated the Tabora Arabs but Tippu Tip had been away, and besides, 'we are brothers', Mirambo's message said. 'I have not forgotten that your grandfather helped my grandfather when he was made chief. I will be happy to receive you, or any of your representatives.' [7]

Tippu Tip couldn't wish for anything better. He admired Mirambo who was more like himself than the normal run of chiefs he had systematically defeated, and despite the Tabora Arabs' remonstrations, he sent a delegation to Urambo. Mirambo himself was away fighting, as his brother informed the visitors, but he had left instructions for the delegates to be welcome and given gifts and slave girls to take back to his friend and brother Tippu Tip.

With Mirambo's assurance of friendship, he decided it was a good time to collect the remaining ivory from Ujiji, and incidentally teach Chief Kasanura of Uvinza that he was not the kind of Arab trader he could rob and intimidate.

[6] Hermann Wissman, *Through Equatorial Africa*.
[7] Murjebi Family Papers.

95

'Nobody has ever cheated me and gone home laughing,' he said to his father who was trying to dissuade him. [7]

Defeating Kasanura was not an easy matter. To begin with he was very well armed, and his village was built on an island in the middle of a stream, surrounded by moats and two very high stockades of thick logs.

On the first day Tippu Tip led a company of his best men to the attack, and they waded the stream waist-deep in water. The villagers let them come close to the stockade and then fired at close range. Tippu Tip escaped injury, but very few of his men returned to camp. Day after day Tippu Tip went to the attack and every day he was repulsed losing a great number of men and guns. Kasanura sent to Mirambo for help, but the great chief refused to join the fight saying he was a friend of Tippu Tip's. As the weeks went by and the losses increased, he decided that his usual methods were of no use against Kasanura's village. He called his carpenters together, sent men to requisition canoes and others to cut down trees, and within a few hours he had a tower on wheels, higher than the Wavinza stockade and filled with the best fighters he had left. The tower was then floated on canoes across the stream and pushed on its wheels close to the stockade. Tippu Tip had never heard of the Greeks or the Romans and their war machines, but his structure was effective enough in Uvinza. The strongly fortified village soon became an inferno of flames and screaming people.

'Those who died, died,' was Tippu Tip's typical summing up. [8] 'The others were made prisoner and a new chief was appointed.'

Now the road to Ujiji was clear. Ruanda and Uvinza had been settled, Mirambo was friendly, and the ivory could be carried in perfect safety.

News of his father's death reached him in Ujiji as he was organising the huge caravan. This came as a shock but being a practical man he didn't waste time, but speeded up the preparations and left the lake for Tabora. Some ten Arab and Swahili traders, including Rumaliza, asked to join Tippu Tip's well guarded caravan. Word of his friendship with Mirambo had travelled fast, and Tippu Tip enjoyed the role of generous protector. He assured them that Mirambo would never molest them if they travelled with him, but even he began to doubt his own faith in Mirambo when some of his guards came running into

[8] Murjebi Family Papers.

camp shouting that Mirambo's men were attacking and they had already taken some prisoners from Tippu Tip's rear guard. There was no time to lose in observation about human nature, but he realised that if Mirambo wanted to, he could wipe out twelve years of hard work in a few hours, and he immediately ordered a stockade built and then waited. Fortunately for him and his hangers on, Mirambo kept his promise, and when the Ruga-Ruga discovered that their prisoners were Tippu Tip's men, they released them and sent them back with apologies.

A week later the great caravan had safely reached Tabora and Tippu Tip immediately went to his stepmother. Just before he had left Tabora, his father, who was old but seemed in the best of health, had said to him: 'Man does not know the date of his death. If I die, look after your mother Nyaso, daughter of Fundi Kira, with both eyes, if you want my blessing.' Tippu Tip had reassured his father. [9] 'By the grace of God, I will do so more than in your lifetime,' and now he intended to keep his promise.

Whilst he was in Tabora, Mirambo sent another invitation for him or his son to visit him in Urambo. Sef begged his father to send him and Tippu Tip agreed to let him go with a small escort and porters to carry the carefully chosen gifts which were most likely to please Mirambo. The porters carried fifty loads which included a number of guns and powder, and young Sef was received at Mirambo's court as an honoured guest, despite the Tabora Arab's efforts to turn the visit into a blood bath. They had been furious when Tippu Tip decided to send his son to pay homage to the man who made their life a misery, so they had sent messengers ahead to warn Mirambo that Sef was bringing a great force from the Sultan of Zanzibar to destroy him. Fortunately for Sef and his party, Mirambo took no notice of the warning and after a few days, he sent Sef back to Tabora with slaves and gifts for Tippu Tip and messages of eternal brotherhood. At least this is what Tippu Tip told Brode many years later.

The German explorer Hermann Wissman, who was in Urambo at the time, tells a slightly different tale. Tippu Tip's son, 'a young man of twenty with a chivalrous bearing, was received politely but as a suppliant,' he says. [10]

Hermann Wissman was the first European to have crossed Africa from West to East, 'for the German flag', as he so patrioti-

[9] *Maisha ya Hamed bin Muhammed el Murjebi, yaani Tippu Tip.*
[10] Hermann von Wissman, *Through Equatorial Africa.*

97

cally put it, and in August 1882, at the time of Sef's visit to Mirambo, he was also a guest of the warrior chief. He described Mirambo as 'tall and of sinewy build, placid, attractive features, and gentle speech'. Mirambo was very hospitable to the traveller and proudly showed him his large arsenal.

A few days later, as Tippu Tip was about to start on the last leg of his journey back to the coast, Wissman arrived in Tabora and asked to join the caravan. Despite his experiences with Stanley, Tippu Tip was delighted for a chance to be of help to another white infidel who had so little left after his long journey. Tippu Tip had to give him provisions and porters, and even pay in slaves, his own precious slaves, to obtain permission from the Wagogo to let the European take water from their wells.

Wissman was of course charmed by Tippu Tip. 'He was a man of about forty five,' he wrote, 'and quite black in complexion, although his father was a pure Arab. Somewhat stout, he is yet very quick in his movements, graceful and polite, decided in his gestures, yet often, like his son, a touch of watchfulness and furtiveness, and seems to be fond of mocking.'

By now Tippu Tip was an experienced handler of European travellers and Stanley had taught him to be watchful. His father was not a pure Arab, of course, but Tippu Tip was not anxious to divulge the truth of his ancestry.

By the end of October 1882, Tippu Tip's caravan of slaves and ivory reached Bagamoyo. Almost exactly six years after Sultan Barghash had issued a proclamation decreeing the abolition of the slave trade and forbidding the transit of new slaves, or raw slaves as they were called. 'Slavery is at an end in all these parts,' Sultan Barghash officially wrote to Consul Kirk in January 1876. 'Inform Lord Derby that we have done it.' [11]

Tippu Tip shared the feeling as he read his Sultan's personal welcoming message to him. He had indeed 'done it'. Once again, and after twelve years in the interior, countless battles, victories, losses and hardships, he had 'done it'. He had brought back to the coast great wealth for himself, his Sultan, his banker and all the others who lived by the selling of 'black and white ivory'. The

[11] To implement his 1876 proclamation prohibiting the slave trade, and on Kirk's advice, Sultan Barghash decided to improve and increase his small and undisciplined army, by hiring a British officer. The man chosen was Lieutenant William Lloyd Mathews of H.M.S. *London*, who was destined to serve under five successive Sultans until his death in 1901.

sale of slaves would be a little more complicated than in the past, but Tippu Tip had no doubt that he would find a way of disposing of them and still make a profit.

He left his goods in the hands of the Indian forwarding agent in Bagamoyo, and he boarded the first dhow sailing for Zanzibar.

CHAPTER TWELVE

The European Schemes and the Sultan's Interests

Tippu Tip's arrival in Zanzibar was anxiously awaited, not because of the wealth he brought to the island, but because Sultan Barghash had decided that the only man who could save his interests between the coast and Lake Tanganyika, was Tippu Tip.

It was Kirk who had suggested to the Sultan that he should empower Tippu Tip with the consolidation of all the territories between the coast and the lake, and had the Sultan done so, he would have prevented the loss of those territories just in time. Two years later the chiefs submitted to the German Protectorate and all the Sultan's protests passed unnoticed because he could not prove that he had ever had sovereignty rights on those districts.

Since leaving Zanzibar twelve years before, a great many things had happened besides the Sultan's final agreement to the abolition of the slave trade. In the 1870s, the major European powers were beginning to take a slow but steady interest in the African continent.

After Livingstone's death a number of evangelical missions had established themselves in the interior, and the missionary penetration, together with the explorers' writings, made Europe suddenly aware of Africa and its great natural resources. It was not long before the missionaries were followed by the scientists and the scientists by the speculators, all of them courting the Sultan of Zanzibar and the local chiefs for special concessions. Political ambitions soon followed. Scientific expeditions, like the German African Society of Berlin, were very politically minded; and the most politically minded of all was the African International Association sponsored by the King of the Belgians, King Leopold.

As Tippu Tip had discovered on his way back to Zanzibar, by 1880 the Association had established a Station at Tabora and one on Lake Tanganyika. Its initial purpose being the suppression of slavery, and 'to assist in the evangelisation of the blacks and the introduction among them of commerce and modern industry', King Leopold had said.

This was a definite threat to the Arab traders, although not immediately realised by the Sultan, the traders themselves, or even Tippu Tip when a few hours after his arrival in Zanzibar he was approached by a Captain Cambier, the representative of the International Association. Tippu Tip had already met Cambier in Tabora, and now the Belgian offered him a share in the administration of the Upper Congo where the Belgians had established yet another station known as Stanley Falls on the Lualaba.

Tippu Tip had already been told by Taria Topan that the Sultan was still very worried about the Arabs' position in Mirambo's Unyamwezi district, and that he was going to offer Tippu Tip the post of Wali of Tabora. 'I am already a great chief in Manyema, why should I want to be a Wali of that small place?' he said to the banker. [1] His answer to Captain Cambier was more specific. 'I am a subject of the Sultan,' he said to the Belgian with all the dignity he could muster. 'And the country of Manyema over which I rule, both it and I are under the authority of Seyyid. I can do nothing without his sanction.'

Early the following morning, the Sultan received Tippu Tip with a great show of affection and immediately explained to him his worries and fears. The Egyptians had tried to occupy his territories along the Somali coast, the Germans and the Belgians were infiltrating, Mirambo was giving trouble, his own subjects on the coastal belt were rebelling against his orders for the abolition of slavery, and the British were pressing him to 'consolidate' his position on the mainland. 'Hamed, you could help me,' the Sultan said to Tippu Tip. [1] 'I want you to take over as Wali of Tabora and look after that district for me.'

'I will be happy to do whatever you ask of me, Seyyid,' Tippu Tip replied, 'but first you must be informed about the Belgians.'

[1] Murjebi Family Papers and *Maisha ya Hamed bin Muhammed el Murjebi, yaani Tippu Tip.*

101

Barghash was shocked when he heard what Tippu Tip had to say about the devious Belgian offer.

He immediately asked Tippu Tip to forget the Wali-ship of Tabora and urged him to return to Manyema 'with all speed, Hamed. You must protect our interests there against these European expansionists' designs.'

Taria Topan was instructed to give Tippu Tip every assistance in recruiting porters, collecting arms and goods. No effort was to be spared in helping him to organise a strong caravan and return to the Upper Congo. No other caravan was to be allowed to recruit porters until Tippu Tip had all he wanted.

However, despite the Sultan's urgent exhortations, it took Tippu Tip a few months to collect what he needed. When he finally left Zanzibar at the end of 1883, he headed the largest caravan ever to leave the island. Apart from tons of goods and stores, he had a thousand guns to defend his dominions and the Sultan's interest, but most of all he appreciated the Sultan's personal gifts to him. 'The Sultan gave me money, clothes, a dagger encrusted with precious stones, a golden scimitar, a diamond ring, a gold watch and two bottles of essence of roses and aloes,' he proudly said to Professor Brode a few years later.

Rumaliza [2] and his brother Nasor, asked to join his caravan again, and although they were not able to raise any capital, Tippu Tip allowed them to go along. 'He was considered a bad risk by everybody,' Tippu Tip said, [3] 'but I felt sorry for him. I should have known better.'

Except for a brief stop with his friend Mirambo who provided him with two hundred porters, he marched on towards the Congo as fast as the huge caravan could move.

Once back in his old territories he felt happier and more relaxed than at any time since he had left. 'The world has gone mad, my son,' he said to Sef who had joined Bwana Nzige at Kasongo. 'Zanzibar is no longer what it used to be. I used to go to Zanzibar to rest and have peace, now I have to come here to find peace.'

Peace was not exactly the right word. Chiefs were still being murdered or deposed or at war with each other, and more and more Arabs had followed in Tippu Tip's footsteps frantically searching for ivory and slaves before the Europeans became too powerful and closed those profitable markets. Tippu Tip's agents

[2] Muhammed bin Khalfan, the trader from Ujiji.
[3] Murjebi Family Papers.

were doing likewise and he was very gratified to see that nothing had really changed except for a few Belgian stations which barely touched the thousands of miles surrounding them.

He decided that as he was now his Sultan's official representative, he should pay a courtesy visit to the Belgian post known as Stanley Falls.

'Named after my friend after I took him there,' Tippu Tip remarked to his son. [4] 'Nobody has named anything after me.'

'There's still time, father,' Sef replied. 'Besides, I was named after you.'

'But never Tippu Tip, whose guns are too terrible to hear,' he laughed and blinked.

He laughed but he made sure that the escort following him for the official visit to the Belgians looked impressive.

Stanley Falls was a strongly fortified station and one of a series in the newly formed Congo Free State, but its presence had not changed the habits of the local tribes. Ninety per cent of a caravan Tippu Tip had sent down the Congo River, 'to look after all manner of things' as Sultan Barghash had instructed him to do, were ambushed and eaten. The Sultan had commissioned him to consolidate and further expand his Upper Congo territories, taking possession of the whole Congo Basin, and prevent the shipment of ivory down the Congo River to the west coast.

A tall order, which Tippu Tip tried to execute but suddenly messages started to arrive from the Sultan ordering him to come back to Zanzibar. The situation was deteriorating faster than any of them had anticipated. The Germans were 'hoisting flags wherever possible', [5] and after Bismarck had sent seven warships to Zanzibar to convince the Sultan that his arguments were groundless, in August 1885 Barghash agreed to the German claims.

England then became involved in the negotiations between Zanzibar and Germany and in 1886 it was agreed that the Sultan should retain the islands of Zanzibar, Pemba, Lamu and Mafia and a ten mile belt on the mainland from the River Rovuma to Kipini. The German East Africa Company obtained a lease from the Sultan for the harbours of Dar es Salaam and Pangani as access to the sea for its territories and so established the first European colonial rule in East Africa.

[4] Murjebi Family Papers.
[5] Carl Peters, *New Light on Dark Africa*, 1891.

At first the Arabs of Tabora had laughed at the crazy Europeans who came through their small outpost in tattered clothes to follow rivers and climb mountains, but by 1886, when Tippu Tip reached Tabora, good humour had turned into open hostility and a German ivory trader, Giesecke, was murdered. Only a few hours before Giesecke had met Tippu Tip and had complained that the Arabs were hostile to him and were trying to murder him. Tippu Tip had agreed to take Giesecke back to the coast together with a Russian, Dr. Junker [6] who had also asked for Tippu Tip's protection. That night Giesecke was shot at again and mortally wounded. Tippu Tip was greatly upset by the shooting. Having accepted Giesecke as a guest in his camp, he felt responsible for him. He arranged for the French missionaries to take care of the dying German, and went off in the middle of the night to remonstrate with the Wali, demanding that the murderer be delivered to him. The murderer was eventually delivered, but not to Tippu Tip, and not until 1890 when he was brought back to the coast and there tried and hanged.

Despite his grandfather's and his father's ties with Tabora, Tippu Tip had never liked the Arabs there, and as soon as he had collected Giesecke's ivory for delivery to his company in Zanzibar, he assembled the caravan and left with Dr. Junker.

Tippu Tip had always been a realist. For years he had watched the Europeans' expansionist manoeuvres and even learnt to live with them. Long ago he had realised that neither he nor the Sultan could fight against the Europeans' overwhelming power, therefore, he was not much surprised when on arrival in Zanzibar the Sultan said to him: [7] 'Hamed, you must forgive me, but I no longer have any hope of keeping the hinterlands. The Europeans here in Zanzibar want to steal everything from me. Those who are dead, who see nothing of this, are at peace. You too are a stranger to it, but soon you will see what is involved.'

'When I heard this, I knew it was all up with us,' Tippu Tip said.

Another man who was disgusted at the turn of events, was the British Consul, Sir John Kirk. Was Britain to sit by and watch Germany take over a whole country which had been in 'the British sphere of influence' for so long? he asked. Like the

[6] Dr. Junker was returning to the coast after failing to reach Emin Pasha in Southern Sudan.
[7] Prof. Heinrich Brode's *Tippu Tip*.

104

Sultan, he felt betrayed on all sides. Britain was too involved with Khartoum and European politics to continue antagonising a great power such as Germany in order to protect a small Sultan, but a Delimitation Commission was eventually set up. The British sent Colonel Kitchener to represent their interests. The other representatives were, Dr. Schmidt for Germany and Monsieur Patrimonio for France. The Sultan was asked to appoint a representative and he chose his army commander, General Mathews. Barghash had complete faith in Mathews, but the general was soon informed by the German representative that he was only required to answer questions—not to state the Sultan's case.

Although the Sultan's tiny army under General Mathews had never made too much of an impression in the interior, a semblance of law and order was maintained, but now with everybody quarrelling as to what belonged to whom, inter-tribal fighting and slave raiding revived, a severe famine swept the country, and once again chiefs sold their subjects and parents their children. Slaves were again brought to the coast in huge numbers. 'I believe,' reported Kirk in 1886, 'the slave traffic to have been greater last year than it has been for some time.' [8]

The Sultan had sent Mathews to try and stop it, 'but that officer had only visited one section where the movement was misrepresented by German agents for political reasons.... So long as rebellion is openly encouraged and the Sultan's right to exercise authority called in question by subjects of European Powers, His Highness is not likely to estrange his people by active steps in a matter that interests us chiefly....' [9]

The work of a lifetime, Kirk's personal fight against slavery, was being destroyed, and his influence on the Sultan no longer required. Bismarck was not pleased with Sir John's role as adviser to the Sultan. It was felt that he was working against German interest and as Britain wanted Germany's support against France over the Egyptian question, Kirk was recalled. He left Zanzibar in July 1886, a sick and disillusioned man.

John Kirk's services to Zanzibar were manifold, but during the twenty years he spent there, first as Agency Surgeon, then as Vice-Consul and finally as Consul, his first loyalty was to the fight for the complete suppression of slavery in the Sultan's dominions.

[8] Anti-Slavery Society Archives.
[9] Public Record Office.

This should have made him the most unpopular man in the whole of East Africa and the adjoining islands, but the fact is that throughout the years as a friend and adviser to Sultan Barghash, he was very well liked even though his policy was not. Although he was on Her Majesty's service, he always did what he thought was best for the interest of Zanzibar, and fighting slavery, was in his opinion not only in the interest of the African on the mainland, but also of the Arabs who would eventually learn to develop their other resources such as gum-copal and cloves, with the help of paid and free labour. The idea was as repulsive and unnatural to an Arab as giving up his harem, but in the end Consul Kirk, with the help of the British Navy, got his way.

However, like the Sultan he had served for so many years, he had to bow to the workings of politics made in Europe, and watch the whole of East and Central Africa being carved up between Germany, Britain, Belgium and Portugal.

Consul Kirk and Sultan Barghash both died defeated men, one in England and one in Zanzibar, within two years of each other.

Tippu Tip was in Zanzibar when John Kirk left, and despite their many clashes, he was very sorry to see him go. 'The last white man who really cared about the fate of our island,' he said. [10]

Soon after his return to Zanzibar, news reached the island that fighting had broken out between the Belgians at Stanley Falls and the Arabs under his cousin Bwana Nzige.

The pretext for the Arab attack on the fort had been one of Tippu Tip's slave women. 'I never liked women with filed teeth', he said. 'Her man-eating habits revolted me, so I gave her to my cousin Nzige who used to beat her regularly.' The woman took refuge in the Belgian fort, and the fight had started. An Englishman by the name of Dean was then in charge of the station's small force. The garrison was totally wiped out and Dean escaped across the river, running from the pursuing Arabs and hiding in the bush for a month until he was rescued by the steamer of the Association International Africaine.

This incident might have meant the end of Tippu Tip's career in the Congo, but suddenly an old travelling companion reappeared in Zanzibar. None other than Henry Morton Stanley, once again engaged on a rescue mission.

A German Jew (converted to Christianity), had been made

[10] Murjebi Family Papers.

Governor of the Equatorial Province belonging to Egypt. His name was Eduard Schnitzer, but he was known as Emin Pasha since becoming an Egyptian Governor. The Mahdi revolt in the Sudan had cut Emin Pasha off from Egypt and as the Egyptians had abandoned all hope of rescuing their Equatorial Province and its Governor, it was left to other parties to organise a relief expedition. Sir William Mackinnon undertook the organisation and Stanley was engaged to lead the expedition. A great deal of money was involved. Much more than in any other expedition Stanley had previously led, and this meant that the best equipment and men were engaged for the purpose. Despite previous unpleasant experiences, Stanley wanted Tippu Tip to join his new venture.

'We wanted the expedition to come direct to the West coast from Europe, but when I heard that you were in Zanzibar, we decided to come to see you,' Stanley said to Tippu Tip when they met at the new British Consul's office.

Tippu Tip was delighted at the opportunity of returning to his old hunting grounds—at Stanley's expense, but at first he played hard to get. He was still furious about the fight between the Belgians and his Arabs at Stanley Falls as he held the Belgians responsible for the whole incident, but the main reason for his apparent lack of initial interest was Stanley himself. Tippu Tip had not forgotten the difficulties of their previous journey together.

CHAPTER THIRTEEN

Helping Stanley Again and Governing the Upper Congo

Stanley had not forgotten either, but he needed Tippu Tip's support to reach Emin Pasha in Southern Sudan. Dr. Junker had tried to reach the Pasha by the Eastern route, but King Mwanga had refused him passage through Uganda and the Russian explorer had to turn back and return to the coast with Tippu Tip. This meant that the only other road open to a rescue team was the Congo.

Stanley had planned to sail from Zanzibar around the Cape to the mouth of the Congo River in West Africa, then up the river which he had explored ten years before;[1] and across to Lake Albert and Southern Sudan. He decided that without the co-operation of the Arabs in the Upper Congo, he would never get through. These were the same Arabs who had recently attacked the fort at Stanley Falls and chased away the Belgians. The only man who could obtain this co-operation was Tippu Tip.

'On arriving in Zanzibar, I found our agent Mr. Edmund Mackenzie was almost ready for embarkation,' Stanley wrote.[2] 'There were a few things to be done however—such as arranging with the famous Tippu-Tib about our line of conduct towards one another. Tippu-Tib is a much greater man today than he was in the year 1877, when he escorted my caravan, preliminary to our descent down the Congo. He has invested his hard-earned fortune in guns and powder. Adventurous Arabs have flocked to

[1] 'When that now famous Arab deserted me in mid Africa', Stanley wrote in his book *In Darkest Africa* referring to his first journey down the River Congo with Tippu Tip.
[2] Quotations in this chapter from Stanley's *In Darkest Africa*.

his standard, until he is now an uncrowned king of the region between Stanley Falls and Tanganyika Lake, commanding many thousands of men inured to fighting and wild Equatorial life. If I discovered hostile intentions, my idea was to give him a wide berth. . . .

'Between Tippu-Tib and Mwanga, King of Uganda, there was only a choice of the frying-pan and the fire. [3] Tippu-Tib was the Zubehr of the Congo Basin—just as formidable if made an enemy, as the latter would have been at the head of his slaves. . . . Therefore, with due caution, I sounded Tippu-Tib on the first day, and found him fully prepared for any eventuality—to fight me, or be employed by me. I chose the latter, and we proceeded to business. His aid was not required to enable me to reach Emin Pasha, or to show the road. There are four good roads to Wadelai from the Congo; one of them was in Tippu-Tib's power, the remaining three are clear of him and his myriads. . . .

'Dr. Junker informed me that Emin Pasha possessed about 75 tons of ivory. So much ivory would amount to £60,000 at 8s. per lb. . . . Why not attempt the carriage of this ivory to the Congo?[4] Accordingly, I wished to engage Tippu-Tib and his people to assist me in conveying the ammunition to Emin Pasha, and on return to carry this ivory. After a good deal of bargaining I entered into a contract with him, by which he agreed to supply 600 carriers at £6 per loaded head. . . .

'On the conclusion of this contract, which was entered in the presence of the British Consul General, I broached another subject in the name of His Majesty King Leopold with Tippu-Tib . . . By the retreat of the officers of the State from Stanley Falls, the floodgates were opened and the Arabs pressed down river. Tippu-Tib being of course the guiding spirit of the Arabs west of Tanganyika Lake, it was advisable to see how far his aid might be secured to check this stream of Arabs from destroying the country. After the interchange of messages by cable [5] with Brussels—on the second day of my stay at Zanzibar—I signed

[3] The mad king had ordered the murder of Bishop Hannington in 1885, and by 1887 the mass slaughter of Uganda Christians was in full swing.

[4] The cost of the expedition was £21,500, and Stanley planned to cover that cost from the sale of the ivory.

[5] Sir William Mackinnon of the British India Company, in 1876 had brought the first steamship service and regular mail to Zanzibar. He was also responsible for the laying of a telegraph cable from Aden.

an engagement with Tippu-Tib by which he was appointed
Governor of Stanley Falls at a regular salary, paid monthly at
Zanzibar, into the British Consul General's hands. His duties
will be principally to defend Stanley Falls in the name of the
State against all Arabs and natives. The flag of the Station will
be that of the State. At all hazards he is to defeat and capture all
persons raiding the territory for slaves, and to disperse all bodies
of men who may be justly suspected of violent designs. He is to
abstain from all slave traffic below the Falls himself, and to
prevent all in his command trading in slaves. In order to ensure
a faithful performance of his engagement with the State, an European officer is to be appointed Resident at the Falls.

'On the breach of any article in the contract being reported,
the salary is to cease.'[6]

Tippu Tip read the agreement slowly and carefully, nodded
and blinked thoughtfully at Stanley and the Consul and said
nothing.

'Hamed, do you understand what that document clearly states?'
the British Consul asked.

'I understand. I understand perfectly,' Tippu Tip replied.

'And what is your answer? Do you agree to the conditions?'
Stanley insisted impatiently.

'I cannot agree to anything until I have consulted the Sultan,'
Tippu Tip replied.

'How can I agree to a miserable thirty pounds a month to
govern a country which is already mine?' he asked the Sultan.

'Hamed go,' the Sultan said. 'Go as far as they want.'[7]

'But for thirty pounds a month ...'

'Even if they offer you ten pounds a month, you must go. I
want you to be there. Besides you can still carry on your business.'

---

[6] Walter Barttelot later published a biography in defence of his brother,
Major Edmund Barttelot who was one of Stanley's officers in command
of the rear column. In that book he states: 'So that by this agreement,
slavery, slave-catching, and pillaging native property were actually
allowed—nay more, countenanced and permitted—to a salaried Governor
appointed by Mr. Stanley and the King of the Belgians over all the
country above Stanley Falls, a vast distance of some hundreds of thousands of square miles, and with a large native population. Of the
value of the agreement not to raid the country below the Falls we have
sad experience. . . .'

[7] *Maisha ya Hamed bin Muhammed el Murjebi, yaani Tippu Tip* and
Murjebi Family Papers.

Which was exactly what Tippu Tip had in mind and intended to do.

The Sultan gave Tippu Tip another diamond ring, a gold watch and 2,000 rupees as parting gifts. They said good-bye and Tippu Tip never saw Barghash again. A year later, on the 18th of March 1888, he died in his palace Bet-el-Ajaid, the House of Wonders. He was only fifty, but as Holmwood, the new British Consul General then wrote, 'he was on the verge of distraction and quite unequal to facing his difficulties'.

Stanley also visited Sultan Barghash before leaving Zanzibar, and he wrote: 'The Sultan of Zanzibar received me with unusual kindness ... he presented me with a fine sword, a shirazy blade I should say, richly mounted with gold, and a magnificent diamond ring, which quite makes Tippu-Tib's eyes water.' They were again competing with each other. Two strong personalities of different background but very similar nature. Neither of them cared too much about the means providing they achieved their ends. Tippu Tip's objective was to return to the Congo, and Stanley's to complete his mission in as short a time as possible.

Tippu Tip had agreed to all of Stanley's proposals, and 'in consideration of these services,' the explorer wrote, 'which Tippu-Tib has solemnly contracted to perform, I permitted him free passage for himself and ninety-six of his kinsmen from Zanzibar to the Congo, with board included. I also undertook the responsibility of conveying the entire party safely to Stanley Falls, to ensure for us a peaceful march from the Congo through his territory, a thing that would have been by no means possible without him. Having bound Tippu-Tib to me I feel somewhat safe against that constant fear of desertion of the Zanzibaris.'

The agents, Smith, Mackenzie & Co., had engaged 600 Zanzibaris on Stanley's behalf, and within three days of his arrival in Zanzibar the famous explorer and his party embarked on the steamer *Madura*.

Besides the *Madura*, two other steamers were engaged: the *Oriental* and the *Navarino* carrying the 600 Zanzibaris, Tippu Tip's contingent which included women, 60 Sudanese and Somali guards, 40 pack donkeys, 10 riding asses and saddles, 27,262 yards of cloth, 6 tons of rice, grain, potatoes, corn and bananas; 1 ton of wire, brass, copper and iron; a 28 foot boat divided in 12 sections of 75 lbs. each; 510 Remington rifles, gunpowder and ammunition; 85,000 cartridges, and a Maxim automatic gun.

Then there were shovels, axes, hoes, medicines, special rain-proof tents, *and* forty carrier loads of Fortnum & Mason's 'choicest provisions' for Stanley and his officers.

Stanley was accompanied by seven Europeans whom he had carefully selected from hundreds of applicants in England. These men were so keen to be included in an African expedition led by the famous explorer, that two of them even paid £1,000 each to be allowed to join. They were Mr. Jephson and Mr. Jameson. The others were: Lt. Stairs, Mr. Bonny, Mr. Troup, Major Barttelot and Captain Nelson. Most of them were young, inexperienced and full of dreams. For all of them the dreams turned into nightmares and hatred for their leader. Barttelot, Jameson and Jephson lost their lives.

Tippu Tip had never travelled on anything but small Arab dhows, but on the 25th February 1887 he boarded the steamer with complete confidence, looking as aristocratic as ever in his white and gold head-dress and flowing robes held fast at the waist by a jewelled dagger and belt. He was a little heavier now, and his beard was almost white, but he was still a powerful man in his early fifties. He was of course impressed with Stanley's organisation and equipment, but if Stanley expected to see the 'uncrowned king' awed by this display of power, he was disappointed. Only on one occasion Tippu Tip expressed anything approaching open admiration.

The first European town he had ever seen was Cape Town and after Stanley had taken him on a tour of the busy port and told him the history of the place, he said: 'Formerly I thought all white men to be fools. Now I think they have something to them. They are more enterprising than Arabs. How much better all these things appear than in Zanzibar. I begin to think you must be very clever.'

Stanley was not aware of any sarcasm in Tippu Tip's voice and he said: 'It is a pity you never went to England for a visit.'

'I hope to go before I die,' was Tippu Tip's dignified reply.

'Be faithful to us on this long journey, and I will take you there, and you will see more things than you can dream of now,' Stanley promised.

'Inshallah! If it is the will of Allah we shall go together,'[8] Tippu Tip smiled and blinked.

Three weeks later they arrived at the mouth of the Congo

[8] H. M. Stanley's *In Darkest Africa*.

River where after some delay, stores and men were transferred to the boats which were to take them up the river to Bangala.

Stanley was a very thorough organiser, and according to his officers, a very bad tempered man when things went wrong. He expected people under his command to follow his instructions to the letter and keep their promises. The two things that worried him most in dealing with Tippu Tip. Remembering their previous experience together, Stanley did not trust Tippu Tip to deliver the 600 porters as he had promised, therefore he had decided to split the expedition in two columns. The first, led by himself, would strike out along the Arwimi River to Lake Albert to reach Emin Pasha as quickly as possible; and the second column, or rear column of 200 men, he left behind under Major Barttelot's command to follow with the greater part of the stores when Tippu Tip returned with the 600 porters he was going to recruit in the Stanley Falls' area.

The success of the Relief Expedition very much depended on Tippu Tip supplying porters, but Stanley maintains that if the instructions he had left Major Barttelot had been followed, there would have been no loss of life, the valuable stores would have been saved and the whole operation could have been carried out in one year instead of the two and half years it took.

From the very beginning relations between Stanley and his second in command, Major Barttelot, were strained. Major Barttelot considered himself 'a gentleman and an officer' and he soon discovered that Stanley, being a self-taught adventurer, had no time for these qualities. 'I'm afraid I may fall short of the mark,' wrote Barttelot to a friend in England at the very beginning of their journey, 'for, of course, and naturally, Stanley expects us to be prodigies in the way and amount of work; but no man can add a cubit to his stature, nor can water ordinarily be squeezed out of a stone. He is a funny chap—Stanley, sometimes I like him fairly well, and sometimes quite the reverse.'

Within two months, the 'reverse' was very much the case. 'Stanley was as usual jumping, shouting and finding fault with everybody,' [9] especially with Major Barttelot whom he threatened to expose as an incompetent coward on their return to England.

Barttelot strongly objected to being left in Tippu Tip's power, and in his diary [10] his dislike for 'that Arab' is very obvious. He

[9] From another letter to the same friend.
[10] The diary was sent back to his brother in England after his death.

found it particularly humiliating to be ordered to accompany Tippu Tip to Stanley Falls on 'a pokey little ship [11] crammed with Tippu-Tib's satellites and women. The smelling women occupying the only cabin,' he wrote.

Stanley was a demanding master, and his orders to Major Barttelot were quite specific—according to Stanley. He was to accompany Tippu Tip to Stanley Falls, then return to Yambuya, a small settlement on one of the Congo confluents, the Arwimi River, and there wait for the rest of the party and provisions to come up from Bangala further down the river; and for Tippu Tip with the 600 porters to come back from Stanley Falls. 'It may happen,' Stanley's orders read, 'that though Tippu-Tib has sent some men, he has not sent enough to carry the goods with your own force. In that case you will, of course, use your discretion as to what goods you can dispense with to enable you to march....'

These orders were issued on the 24th of June, 1887. By the 15th of August Tippu Tip had not sent a single man.

Despite much speculation and writings, nobody has ever been able to give a final answer for Barttelot's interpretation of Stanley's orders. All through his diary Barttelot of course insisted that Stanley had left them without adequate supplies, that porters and askaries were dying or deserting or being eaten by the cannibals; but above all he repeats that Tippu Tip had let them down.

As always, time meant absolutely nothing to Tippu Tip. He was once again comfortably installed at Kasongo and business went on as usual. Of course, he regularly visited Stanley Falls to show the Belgian Resident that he was earning his thirty pounds a month, but there was so much to do and territory to cover, that the demands of the Europeans at Yambuya would have to wait.

Meanwhile Barttelot and Jameson spent their time sending messages and personally chasing Tippu Tip at Stanley Falls and Kasongo. [12] When he was in residence Tippu Tip always impressed his exasperated guests with his wonderful hospitality, and on each occasion he had some very good reason why he hadn't supplied the promised porters as yet, but slowly he convinced the gullible Barttelot that it was really Stanley's own fault if he

[11] The *Henry Reid.*
[12] A distance of 500 miles and 25 days by canoe.

114

couldn't provide the porters. Stanley had failed to fulfil his side of the contract.

'If I had known what he (Stanley) was, and how he was going to treat us, I would never have come,' Barttelot confided to his diary after a long talk with Tippu Tip. 'Part of the agreement on which Tippu-Tib was to let him have the men was, that on arrival here he should supply them with caps and powder. These have all been left behind, and Tippu-Tib knows it. When I was at the Falls Tippu told me he thought Stanley had broken faith with him, and that the men would not come till ammunition arrived. If Tippu-Tib does not send the men, he (Stanley) will be the laughing stock of everybody, because he brought Tippu-Tib round from Zanzibar with a huge following, at tremendous expense, and fed him, and he took up room on the steamer here which would have been more than sufficient to bring up all our men and goods left behind, and instead of there being a camp here, we should all have gone on.... In the meantime, here we are, among the greatest savages in the world, and about the only cannibals left. They look with longing eyes at Jameson and me; they think that, fattened and stuffed with bananas, we should be ripping!'

Even though he blamed Stanley for Tippu Tip's failure to supply the porters, he still couldn't see why as powerful a man as the Governor of the Upper Congo was unable to get together enough porters to help them out of their predicament. 'All the villages under his government are in most excellent order, and their services are always at his disposal,' Barttelot wrote. 'All disputes are laid before Tippu; all villages are laid under a contribution to Tippu as follows: three out of every four tusks of ivory they get. Of course, this only refers to those villages which acknowledge his supremacy; those which do not, he captures all their women and kills as many of the men as he can, the women having to be ransomed for ivory. A short period of this treatment generally brings them into subjection, for though they may move as fast as they like, they are always in the end hunted down and killed....'

On the other hand, Tippu Tip, the man of action, had no time for the helpless Europeans at Yambuya. 'They are young, they are strong, they have guns and men, and all they do is cry to me. I have already done all I can for them.'[13]

[13] Murjebi Family Papers.

By this he meant that he had sent 250 men, 'whom I cannot use, as they are not to be handed over till Tippu himself arrives!' Barttelot wrote to his brother-in-law, in a fury of frustration.

And so the months dragged on, punctuated by the visits to Stanley Falls and Kasongo in search of the elusive Tippu Tip and the promised porters. Meanwhile his own people got sick and died at an alarming rate and as the stores decreased, more and more of the original contingent from Zanzibar deserted to the surrounding Arab settlements.

Major Barttelot's camp at Yambuya was surrounded by a large number of Arab strongholds and Manyema villages, and although he ran it with military discipline, the surrounding Arabs, and particularly Tippu Tip's nephew Salem Mohammed, delighted in disrupting it. The Arabs had no love for the interfering Major who sided with and protected the local villagers, and the young Major strongly objected to being left by Stanley 'completely in the hands of the minions of Tippu-Tib'. Salem was the instigator of the continual pilferage of stores and on one occasion he even threatened Barttelot's life. 'Many, many times I have averted war with the Arabs by eating simple dirt ...' he wrote.

Finally, almost a year after Stanley's departure Tippu Tip delivered 400 porters, not 600 as promised, but although the agreed weight per carrier was 60 lbs., he was absolutely adamant about the weight. Three hundred of his men would carry loads of 40 lbs., and the rest 20 lbs. each and an Arab headman appointed by him was to be paid £1000. Barttelot had no choice but to agree and departure was once more delayed by the weighing and splitting of loads. Even so Tippu Tip was not satisfied. Some of the loads weighed 42 lbs., not 40 as stipulated. More unpacking and more delays. Barttelot's friend and second in command, Lt. Jameson wrote in his diary: 'He was a straightforward, honest English gentleman—his only fault was that he was a little quick-tempered. He loved plain straightforward dealing far too much to get on well with the Arabs.'[14]

Having agreed to every demand, the caravan left Yambuya on the 11th June, but not before Tippu Tip had told his porters that if they had any trouble with Barttelot they should shoot him.[15]

'I would have wagered he (Barttelot) would have seized that

[14] James S. Jameson, *The Story of the Rear Column*, 1890.
[15] A Belgian officer and Mr. Troup (another European left by Stanley with Barttelot) later confirmed this.

flowing gray beard of Tippu-Tib and pounded the face to pulp, even in the midst of his power, rather than allow himself to be thus cajoled time and time again,' Stanley wrote.

Poor Barttelot was hardly in a position to pound anybody's face to a pulp. Even the Belgian officers stationed in the Upper Congo seemed powerless in Tippu Tip's hands. For all his signing of official documents to the effect that he would 'abstain from all slave traffic', Tippu Tip and his satellites were more than ever busy in raiding and expanding. In fact, Stanley was indirectly responsible for some of this expansion as the Arabs raided wherever he had opened new trails.

From the very start Barttelot's newly assembled caravan suffered from desertions, loss of loads and guns. Despite the strict discipline he tried to enforce, there was little he could do to control Tippu Tip's unruly mob, and finally, only a few days after they had started, he left Mr. Bonny in charge of their camp at Banalya and by forced marches reached Stanley Falls to appeal to Tippu Tip for help. He wanted chains and an order for the local chief to supply food for the caravan.

Tippu Tip showed great concern and of course gave Barttelot all he asked for, even 'power of life and death over the Manyema', Barttelot says. Tippu Tip didn't really care what the Major did with the Manyema, he just wanted to be rid of him. Within six days Barttelot was back with the caravan, but not for long.

On the 18th July, the morning after he arrived in camp, he was shot and killed by a Manyema head-porter. He had given orders for the usual and aimless shooting and playing of drums to stop. He was exhausted and irritable after a six days' march and when the drumming and shooting started again, he went himself to see that his orders were obeyed, but as he pushed through a crowd of Manyema surrounding a woman beating on a drum, he was shot by the woman's husband.

At the time Bonny was the only other white man in camp as Jameson, the second in command, was away rustling up deserters, and the resulting chaos after the shooting nearly cost Bonny his life.

When eventually Jameson heard of the murder and on information followed the culprit to Stanley Falls, Tippu Tip showed great regret at the death of such 'a brave officer'. Within a few days, Sanga, Barttelot's murderer was caught by Tippu Tip's men and executed by the Belgian authorities. All somewhat contradictory if indeed he had told the porters to shoot Barttelot at the first sign of trouble. Tippu Tip later of course denied all accusations and insisted that far from instigating the murder, he had ordered the porters, on pain of death, to follow and obey the Europeans at all times.

In Stanley Falls Jameson tried to persuade Tippu Tip to accompany the expedition but although Tippu Tip never asked anybody permission for anything, on this occasion he asked the Belgian representative if he could follow Jameson. A rather startled Belgian refused on the grounds that he would have to obtain official authority from Belgium. Frustrated, sick and at a loss for what to do next, Jameson left Stanley Falls for Bangala, [16] and a few days later he was dead. [17]

In his memoirs, Tippu Tip barely touches on all these events, but he is most emphatic about his good intentions in supplying the 500 (not 600!) porters as promised to Stanley, and he disclaims all responsibility for the many tragedies and failures of the expedition. In fact, when reading Tippu Tip's account, one is under the impression that only a few weeks elapsed between Stanley's departure from Yambuya and the arrival of the porters a year later. For a start, he says, Stanley never sent him the powder he promised and which was needed for the escort of the porters; and secondly when Tippu Tip gave orders for the caravan of porters to go to Yambuya, he himself had to leave Stanley Falls on 'Belgian government business'.

Tippu Tip very much enjoyed his new role of Governor on behalf of a European power. He had been instructed to 'plant' Belgian flags all along the Congo Basin, and this he did conscientiously wherever he went, despite the fact that the country 'was mine by right', he says. He also maintained strict law and order, and by imposing his will on the other Arabs, they all found a 'modus vivendi' with the Belgians, meanwhile accelerating their trading.

Tippu Tip had made up his mind that coming to terms with the Europeans would eventually become a necessary evil, therefore, it was vital for him, his fellow Arabs and the African chiefs associated with the Arab trading system, to collect as much ivory

[16] The nearest point on the Congo River where he could send a telegram to London asking for instructions.
[17] As every other white man, Jameson suffered from malaria, dysentery and malnutrition.

and slaves as possible in as short a time as possible. As he explained to Rumaliza, his partner in Ujiji: 'Our power lies with the Sultan, and even he is following the commands of the Europeans.'[18]

Slavery was still big business in the Congo Free State and tales of this miserable trade are told by all the writers of that period. Between 1880 and 1890 there were more slaves bought and sold in the Upper Congo than at any other time before. The whole political and economic system had changed during those early years of European infiltration. The 'European Interference' and the resulting abolition of the slave trade on the coast, together with the effect of continual wars and famine, made slaves cheap and plentiful in the interior. Slaves were now essential as barter goods instead of beads and cloth. They were also used instead of paid porters, and sometimes to feed the hungry raiding forces. Some of the most horrifying accounts of the cruelty of slavery were written during that last decade when the Arabs realised that their trading paradise was coming to an end, or perhaps the cruelty only *seems* more horrifying because it was better observed by the ever-increasing number of agents for European powers, rescuers of stranded Pashas, and missionaries.

[18] Murjebi Family Papers.

CHAPTER FOURTEEN

Twenty Years After Livingstone—the Threat of Missionary Fervour

By the beginning of the 1880s Stanley Falls had become the most important European trading centre in Central Africa and 'it was full of Europeans', Tippu Tip says. 'It had become a great harbour, and anything you wanted was available there. The Europeans came up the Congo River in boats and left with full loads of ivory.' [1]

Lake Tanganyika, on the other hand, was the missionary centre, and also the principal bone of contention between the Belgians, the Germans and the British.

The British dream was to acquire a strip of land along the lake, which would eventually give them a clear road from Cape to Cairo, and both Tippu Tip and his partner Rumaliza, [2] used their influence with the local chiefs to obtain treaties on behalf of the British. Developments in Europe soon put a stop to the British dream and Lake Tanganyika went to Germany.

Tippu Tip had no illusions as to the inevitability of a complete take-over by one of the European powers. All he was interested in was his commercial future. Rumaliza, on the other hand wanted to be appointed governor of the Lake Tanganyika region on behalf of the British, in the same way as Tippu Tip had been appointed governor of the Congo Free State for the Belgians.

Both Arabs felt that the British might be easier to deal with than the Germans who had already demonstrated their colonising methods by hanging any recalcitrant Arab or African.

In the words of Carl Peters, the original German 'treaty-

[1] Murjebi Family Papers.
[2] The word roughly means, 'the one who utterly finishes'.

maker': '(They) shall have peace,' he said. 'It shall be eternal peace. I will show the Wagogo what the Germans are ... Plunder the village, set fire to the houses, and smash everything to pieces that will not burn.' [3] And all because the son of a local chief had 'grinned impudently' at Peters as he ate his breakfast. Peters repeated this kind of lesson to anybody who obstructed his progress before and after his government acknowledged him as their legal representative. [4]

Whatever the reason, both Tippu Tip and Rumaliza were surprisingly courteous and helpful to the British missionaries in the lake region. The most surprising aspect of the situation was the friendship between Alfred Swann of the London Missionary Society and the Mohammedan slavers.

The missionaries had chosen Ujiji and later Mtowa on the west coast of the lake, for the express purpose of striking at the slave traders by blocking their routes to the East African coast, and of course the leaders of that trade were Tippu Tip and Rumaliza.

The London Missionary Society had employed Alfred Swann, 'A lay missionary/mariner' in 1882 to transport, assemble and then run the first missionary boat on Lake Tanganyika. 'In the midst of their (the Arabs) vile operations it was our fixed determination to live, and in time, to undermine or destroy their diabolical trade in human souls and bodies,' [5] wrote the enthusiastic missionary.

It would have been natural, therefore, for Alfred Swann and the Arabs at least to dislike each other; but Rumaliza, fully supported by Tippu Tip, elected himself the protector of the London Missionary Society mission and Swann greatly appreciated Rumaliza's friendship. Like his superior, Hore, he believed in peaceful co-existence with the Arabs.

[3] Dr. Carl Peters, *New Light on Dark Africa*, 1891.

[4] Without official recognition Peters founded the Society for German Colonization and with three other members of the society, within five weeks had obtained 'crosses' on treaties drawn up by him, from twelve chiefs, who without understanding the meaning of it, handed over their territories without a murmur. Having been given territories twice the size of Germany, the Kaiser was eventually 'pleased' to take them 'under imperial protection'.

[5] Alfred J. Swann, *Fighting the Slave Hunters in Central Africa*, 1890.

The London Missionary Society boat was named the *Morning Star*.

Swann arrived in Zanzibar fired with missionary zeal to destroy slavery, but he was immediately shocked by the evidence of slaves being 'bought and sold both at Zanzibar and on the East Coast. In fact, during our stay on the island,' he wrote, 'a pinnace of H.M.S. London captured as a prize a large slave-dhow which had anchored under the very shadow of the British Consulate—so daring were the Arabs at this exceedingly profitable game.'

He was again shocked when he realised that the porters who would carry his loads and the sections of the boat, were slaves. 'Every man of them was a slave, even the head-men were slaves, and part of their three-months' advanced wages had already gone into the hands of their masters at Zanzibar.'

Tippu Tip would have said that they were not slaves. They were hired porters—hired from their masters, but hired porters —and he would have added that the Europeans never understood the difference between a domestic slave who was treated like one of the family, and a slave in the interior who was just an object of barter.

Whatever their status, Swann's porter/slaves were a cheerful lot, he discovered. Swann had devised a new method of transportation in Africa. He had loaded the boat sections on carts and covered the 820 miles to Ujiji in one hundred and three days. A record, considering that even Stanley took seven months to reach Ujiji when he went to Livingstone's rescue.

Swann's next encounter with slaves was at Mpwapwa, 200 miles from the coast, and these belonged to Tippu Tip. 'Here we met the notorious Tip-pu-Tib's [6] annual caravan, which had been resting after the long march through Ugogo and the passes of Chunyo. As they filed past we noticed many chained by the neck. Others had their necks fastened into the forks of poles about six feet long, the end of which were supported by the men who preceded them. The women, who were as numerous as the men, carried babies on their backs in additional to a tusk of ivory or other burden on their heads. They looked at us with suspicion and fear, having been told, as we subsequently ascertained, that white men always desired the release of slaves in order to eat their flesh, like the Upper Congo cannibals,' he wrote.

[6] Yet another spelling of the name. On that occasion Swann missed Tippu Tip himself by a few days. Tippu Tip was going back to Zanzibar after twelve years in the interior.

'It is difficult adequately to describe the filthy state of their bodies; in many instances, not only scarred by the cut of a 'chikote' (a piece of hide used to enforce obedience), but feet and shoulders were a mass of open sores, made more painful by the swarms of flies which followed the march and lived on the flowing blood. They presented a moving picture of utter misery, and one could not help wondering how any of them had survived the long tramp from the Upper Congo, at least 1000 miles distant. Our own inconveniences sank into insignificance compared with the suffering of this crowd of half-starved, ill-treated creatures who, weary and friendless, must have longed for death.

'The head-men in charge were most polite to us as they passed our camp. Each was armed with a rifle, a knife, and spear, and although decently clothed in clean cotton garments, they presented a thoroughly villainous appearance.

'Addressing one, I pointed out that many of the slaves were unfit to carry loads. To this he smilingly replied: "They have no choice! They must go, or die!" Then ensued the following conversation:- "Are all these slaves destined for Zanzibar?" "Most of them, the remainder will stay at the coast." "Have you lost many on the road?" "Yes! Numbers have died of hunger!" "Any run away?" "No, they are too well guarded. Only those who become possessed with the devil try to escape; there is nowhere they could run to if they should go." "What do you do when they become too ill to travel?" "Spear them at once!" was the fiendish reply. "For, if we did not, others would pretend they were ill in order to avoid carrying their loads. No! We never leave them alive on the road; they all know our custom". "I see women carrying not only a child on their backs, but in addition, a tusk of ivory or other burden on their heads. What do you do in their case when they become too weak to carry both child and ivory? Who carries the ivory?" "She does! We cannot leave valuable ivory on the road. We spear the child and make her burden lighter. Ivory first, child afterwards!" '

Like Livingstone twenty years before, Swann says, 'every humane feeling within me rose in rebellion', but like that other missionary he was unable to help, except for sending 'indignant protests to Zanzibar and England'.

The situation had not changed very much in the twenty years since Livingstone appealing to the world, wrote: 'Besides those actually captured, thousands are killed, or die of their wounds and famine, driven from their homes by the slave-raiders. Thousands perish in internecine wars, waged for slaves with their own clansmen or neighbours; slain by the lust for gain which is stimulated by the slave-purchasers. The many skeletons we have seen amongst the rocks and woods, by the pools, and along the paths, of the wilderness, all testify to the awful sacrifice of human life which must be attributed directly or indirectly to this trade of hell.'[7]

As many other travellers did, Swann met Mirambo in Unyamwezi and was much interested in the leader of the Ruga-Ruga. 'He was tall, stately, and looked every inch a chief,' he wrote. 'We found him upright, manly, great, and years of close contact with him proved him to be loyal to all who merited his friendship.'

Mirambo was fascinated with the carts and the boat sections. When he was told that the sections would be assembled on the lake, he said: 'It is good work. The lake is large. I shall call it my boat, and you can ferry my men across with my ivory as they come from the Congo.'

No less a clever politician than his friend Tippu Tip, Mirambo knew how to deal with romantic missionaries. He agreed with Swann that slavery was an 'abomination' and told him that his only reason for being 'frequently at war' was because he hated the Arab method of undermining the chiefs' authority, inciting the people to fight and then enslaving them. Swann was well satisfied with Mirambo's reactions and if only the Africans could be 'taught that it is not simply a *misfortune* to become a slave, but a real *disgrace*', there was hope, he said. It was not long after this meeting that Mirambo died and what he had built up around his strong personality soon disintegrated.

As everywhere else the arrival of Swann's caravan, with its 'human donkeys dragging the boat's sections on carts', caused quite a stir among the local population of Ujiji, and as customary, he was greeted by firing of guns and beating of drums; somewhat reminiscent of Stanley's arrival when he went to meet Livingstone in 1872. [8]

'Ujiji town was really ruled by the Arabs,' Swann wrote,

[7] David Livingstone's *Last Journals*.
[8] At the time of Swann's arrival, the Arabs still referred to Livingstone as Baba Daud (Father David), and Stanley as Bula Matali (the Stone Breaker). Stanley earned that nickname because of all the rocks he had to blast in the Congo to clear the river for navigation.

'although a native chief was nominally its head. Most of the powerful and wealthy Arabs lived here, superintending the transport of ivory and slaves which came from the West. Both the famous Tip-pu-Tib and his partner, Rumaliza, had their principal homes in the town ... At this powerful centre of trade we were nothing less than guests of the Arabs. Mighty merchant princes, who lived in a curious mixture of luxury and squalor, invited us to tiffin. One walked over tusks of ivory scattered about their courtyards representing thousands of pounds. Diseased slaves moved about in close proximity to gaudily clothed women of the household. The slave-chain and its captives were in evidence everywhere, whilst brutal half-caste fighting men lounged about the verandahs of the most wealthy.'

Hermann Wissman who travelled with Tippu Tip from Tabora to the coast in 1882, and eventually became Imperial Commissioner of the new German colony, often refers to the brutality of the 'half-blood brute who seems to have inherited only the worst qualities of the two tribes to whom he owes his existence'. [9] According to him Tippu Tip himself would have never indulged in so much cruelty as his half-caste subordinates.

Swann goes on describing Ujiji as 'a whited sepulchre, presided over by smooth-talking, clean, perfumed, and polite Arabs, who, in their conduct towards us, were always courteous and generous. Out of respect for us the slave-market was abolished, although active slave-trading was carried on in the town. Strolling along the sands one evening I came upon eight dying slaves, who where suffering from smallpox. They were beyond hope, and had been placed close to the water so that crocodiles might carry them off when the sun set. No one was allowed to go near them under penalty of being shot by a soldier who kept guard. I passed three other bodies partly eaten by hyenas. It was the usual manner of getting rid of slaves who were of no value.

'To a young Arab who accompanied me, I remarked: "Why don't you endeavour to cure the smallpox and save the life?" "Oh!" replied he, with a shrug of the shoulders, "it's not worth it. They are Pagans, and we have had all the expense and trouble of bringing them from the Congo for nothing. Who will carry their load of ivory to the coast?" Ivory! Always ivory! What a curse the elephant has been to Africans. By himself the slave

[9] Hermann Wissman, *Through Equatorial Africa*.

did not pay to transport, but plus ivory he was a paying game.'[10]

Slavery was a paying game to all concerned and the Africans dealing in slaves resented the missionary interference as much as the Arabs. During one of the Arabs' raids quite close to the mission, a number of people took refuge within the mission compound and food supplies were running short. Canoes from a richer tribe further up the lake, floated past the station filled with grain, but they refused to sell to the missionaries. They were on their way to barter with the Arabs, and three days later they passed again on their way home, loaded with young boys and girls. Sixty pounds of grain for a boy and 120 for a girl. 'Old men and women were not marketable, as they could not march to Zanzibar,' Swann says.

Despite petty obstacles placed in their way by Mwinyi Kheri, the Sultan's representative in Ujiji, the London Missionary Society now had a boat on the lake. Alfred Swann and his assistants had assembled and launched the *Morning Star* and were waiting for the components of the first steamer, *Good News*. At least, he says it was the first steamer, but in actual fact the Belgians had been operating the steamer *Cambier* for two years before the *Good News* was launched.

Three months had elapsed since Swann's arrival, and despite the customary courtesies, 'diplomatic swords' were beginning to be crossed between the missionaries and the Arabs. The latter were still reassuring the missionaries that they were anxious to protect them from the 'wild natives', but Swann knew better. 'An Arab, like a lion,' he says, 'is most dangerous when silently stalking his prey. With his curved dagger drawn, and his tongue hurling threats at you, he is not half so near to cutting your throat as when protesting eternal friendship. Secret conferences, we know, were being held at night in their enclosures. Some presentiment of danger disturbed their hitherto serene monopoly of the traffic in humanity. This steel boat must be a small man-o'-war, intended to destroy the slave dhows.'

The time had come to look for a better site for the mission. Swann and his chief, Hore, were against a move as they felt

---

[10] Like many new-comers before and after him, Alfred Swann knew very little of African customs. The dying slaves were left for the crocodiles in the same way as the Africans themselves left their dead and dying for the wild animals to finish off. A most effective way of getting rid of corpses and keeping Africa clean.

that the Catholics would soon 'occupy' what they considered their territory, but the L.M.S. committee ordered them to look for a more strategic spot than the Arab dominated Ujiji. Kavala Island, on the west coast of the lake, and on the main slave-route from Manyema, was chosen. From there they made what they felt to be futile attempts at checking the Arabs in their ever-increasing raids on the neighbouring tribes. The missionaries' frustration is evident from the accounts they wrote of their work. They were so short of men and materials that Swann had to make rivets for the new steamer himself. They were plagued by disease and two young members of the mission died almost as soon as they reached Kavala. Two of Swann's children died of dysentery. The first, a few months' old baby, died on the journey from the coast to Ujiji when Swann was returning from England with new recruits for the mission and a new bride and baby.

All these tragedies they learnt to accept and live with, but the Arabs and their desperate attempts at remaining the masters of the lake and the slave-supplying areas beyond, were unacceptable. Even so, Tippu Tip and Rumaliza were determined to remain on friendly terms with the missionaries, despite the latter's efforts to obstruct their trade. The missionaries, for their part, believed that peaceful co-existence with the Arabs would eventually bring about better results than an out and out war, besides the fact that they well realised their physical inability to fight the Arabs.

Not all the Arabs felt the same about the missionaries. The followers of Mwinyi Kheri were all in favour of putting an end to all missionary interference, both Catholic and L.M.S.; but the Catholics had the protection of the Belgian army station at Karema, and therefore were less likely to be defeated; whereas the undefended L.M.S. were quite open to attack—except that they were under Tippu Tip's and Rumaliza's protection. At least in one instance the slave-traders saved Swann, his wife and the new recruits as they returned to Ujiji from England.

As the caravan approached Ujiji at the end of the 800 miles journey, Swann noticed an unusual silence about the place. The crowds of cheering, shooting, and present bearing Arabs and Africans, who greeting all caravans arriving from the coast, were strangely absent this time. His own Mohammedan servants, he had noticed, had behaved mysteriously for some time and two messengers he sent into town to advise the Arabs of their arrival, never came back. Swann shared his suspicions with the new doctor he was bringing to the lake, but asked him not to say anything to his wife, who was still shaken by the loss of her baby and her first walk across Africa.

They had reached the centre of town when one of the Rumaliza's head-men approached him and said: 'Follow and I will show you where to sleep.' Without question they followed and were shown into a courtyard surrounded by high walls, but once inside Swann wanted an explanation. The head-man answered in the usual evasive Arab manner and asked them to stay in the court-yard and not walk about town. Swann was afraid they had been trapped, but he was still confident that his friend Rumaliza would protect them from any harm. At ten o'clock that night the head-man came back to escort him to Rumaliza.

' "My master wishes to speak to you alone," he said to Swann. "Tell your people to keep the doors closed until you return. Hyenas prowl about at night and bite men." ' The missionary knew what that meant and his fears increased. ' "Small birds tell the buffalo the hunter is near," ' the messenger added mysteri-ously as they entered another courtyard and proceeded down corridors dimly lit by palm-oil lamps. They passed through a beautifully carved entrance and the door was quietly opened by an unseen hand. Swann knew they had entered Rumaliza's harem. ' "Wait where you are until some one comes," the messenger whispered retreating. "When I have closed the door, give the usual salutation. I must not see the women." '

Two small lamps lit the large unfurnished room. Only a beauti-fully worked prayer mat hung on a wall, and Swann realised he was standing in Rumaliza's private devotions' room.

' "Hodi," Swann called out. This is equivalent to our ringing the door bell, and is for the purpose of warning the inmates of your entrance. Unless an answer is returned it is extremely bad manners to advance.

' "Hodini, hodini, Karibu, Bwana! (come in, sir, you are wel-come)", a female voice replied.

'With a light step a beautiful young girl, about fifteen years of age, approached, clad in rich clothes thrown gracefully over her shoulders. The draught carried towards me a delicious perfume, of which these Eastern women are fond,' the romantic missionary wrote in his memoirs. He followed the girl through other rooms and into a well furnished apartment. The girl showed him to a soft sofa covered in cushions and carpets, saying: ' "Master will be with you at once; he is having his bath."

'I was not kept waiting long,' Swann says. 'Rumaliza came in quickly, leaving his sandals outside, and with a smile held out his hand, giving the usual Arab welcome. A lovely woman brought a bowl of water for me to wash my hands, another sprinkled scent over my handkerchief, a third placed hot coffee and cakes at our feet.... Telling the girls to leave us, Rumaliza commenced asking questions about our journey. Who was with me, what we had brought, what news about the war. I wondered when he was going to get to real talk, as no Arab would dream of inviting a Christian into his harem at night without some extraordinary reason. Certainly not simply to be waited on by its inmates, or to gossip about ordinary topics.

'The meal was soon over, the scented dark damsels were called to remove the utensils, and as they passed out, handed us a light fan to keep away mosquitoes. It was all very picturesque, quiet, clean, Oriental, and in its way, fascinating.'

After one or two polite exchanges, Rumaliza finally produced a letter. ' "Can you read Arabic?" ' he asked.

' "No, but if you translate it into Kisuahili, I shall understand it," ' Swann replied.

' "This letter," ' Rumaliza continued, ' "came to me ten days ago. I was then two hundred miles from here. I have been travelling as fast as I could, so as to arrive at the same time as yourself, or before, if possible. It is from Tippu Tip, my partner, who is now on the Congo. These Ujiji Arabs have lost a great deal of property at the coast, in the war against the Germans, and many of their relatives have been killed. In order to be revenged, they decided to intercept your party at the last river and to kill you all. The calico was to be equally divided between them. Your arms and ammunition were to come to me, whilst the vessels on the lake were to become the property of Tippu Tip. On receipt of this news Tippu Tip sent special messengers to me, requesting that I would at once go to Ujiji, stop all this nonsense, and inform these Arabs that if they would not listen to me, I was to place myself and people on your side, and together with his retainers, defend you and your property. I only arrived yesterday at your station, persuaded the white man to give me a passage here, stopped as we passed Ujiji, and sent on shore my messenger, who only reached the Arabs just in time to stop their action." '

Swann was astonished and he asked why Rumaliza and Tippu

Tip were so concerned about him and his party.

'"Because we have no quarrel with you,"' Rumaliza replied. '"We have assisted every Christian traveller who has been to Ujiji. If these Arabs had killed you, there would have been much trouble."'

The story was probably true or possibly fabricated by Rumaliza to keep the missionaries on his side, but Swann wanted to believe it. 'I think the most bitter enemies of the Arabs will acknowledge that this intervention of Tip-pu-Tib and Rumaliza was worthy of all praise,' he wrote. 'It is seldom that a Mohammedan takes sides against his co-religionists in favour of Christians, and it was the more remarkable if we remember that none of us had any special claim on their protection. Nor could blame have rested on these men, had the plot been successful, as they were both hundreds of miles distant at the time.'

Swann was probably very gullible and easily influenced, but the fact remains that Rumaliza and Tippu Tip went on proving their friendship and giving the missionaries their protection until the very end.

CHAPTER FIFTEEN

Legal Action and Dark Clouds

Meanwhile Stanley was still engaged in the rescue of Emin Pasha from Kawalli on the west shore of Lake Albert Nyanza. His rear column was all but disrupted after Major Barttelot's murder and Jameson's death, but he carried on with the few survivors, and although he finally persuaded the Pasha to be 'rescued'; he held Tippu Tip responsible for all his misfortunes. According to Stanley the loss of lives, stores and time was all due to Tippu Tip's failure to supply the promised porters, and whatever Tippu Tip's excuses were, 'He may tell them to the Marines,' Stanley said.

His rage against Tippu Tip did not stop at words. In December 1889 he finally deposited the recalcitrant Emin Pasha with the German authorities in Bagamoyo, where the once German Jewish doctor, turned Christian adventurer, turned Mohammedan Egyptian Pasha, was feasted as a hero. [1] Unfortunately, being short sighted, he fell out of a window during a banquet given in his honour and fractured his skull. However, after his recovery he was made the Imperial Commissioner of the new German colony.

Stanley was anxious about the Pasha's health, but the German refused to see his rescuer again and Stanley proceeded to Zanzibar and there took legal action against Tippu Tip. He found

[1] Instigated by Carl Peters, for political reasons and a covetous eye on Uganda, a strong feeling of patriotic concern for their 'fellow countryman', was whipped up; and a German Emin Pasha Relief Committee collected £20,000 for an expedition to rescue the stranded Governor of Equatoria. However, Stanley, who had been sent by the British Committee for the rescue (headed by Sir William Mackinnon with much about the same political views in mind as Carl Peters), was first to reach the Pasha.

out that the banker Taria Topan was holding some £10,000 for Tippu Tip, and he asked for an injunction on this money by the Zanzibar Consular Court, until such time as Tippu Tip himself was recalled by the Sultan to come to Zanzibar and face the charges.

The recall was not long in coming. The last of the independent rulers of Zanzibar and Tippu Tip's friend, Sultan Barghash had died and when finally the news reached Tippu Tip in distant Stanley Falls, he sent his assurance of loyalty to the new ruler, Sultan Khalifa. All he got for an answer was an order to report back to Zanzibar immediately.

He had been governor of the Congo Free State for two and a half years. 'Life was very good in Stanley Falls,' he said.[2] 'As good as in Zanzibar. Trade was wonderful, and the number of tusks coming in was staggering.'

He had the respect and the support of the Belgian authorities and he enjoyed his role as peace-maker between the Arabs and the Europeans. 'But of course, Stanley had to make trouble as usual,' he said.[2]

When the Sultan's order to report back to Zanzibar arrived, his friends, his relatives, aides, chiefs and dependents, all advised him to ignore the order. 'Are you not stronger than any sultan?' they asked.[2] 'You have thousands of slaves to defend you. Let them take your possessions in Zanzibar. It's better than losing your freedom and all this.'

'You are a lot of fools,' Tippu Tip replied. 'You must be dreaming if you think that a few Arabs and an army of undisciplined savages can fight the power of Europe. Have you already forgotten how easy it was for me to defeat these savages and their great chiefs? How can I now believe that these people are able to defend me?'

'But the Sultan....'

'The Sultan can do nothing,' he cut in sharply. 'The Sultan is in the same position as all of us Arabs. The white man is in his house and he must do as he is told.'

Even the Europeans were sorry to see him go. They realised that without him the Arabs and the chiefs allied to them would start giving trouble again. Although they disapproved of his

[2] Murjebi Family Papers.

methods, at least they had had peace for the past two and half years.

Wherever he passed on his way back to the lake, the Arabs tried to dissuade him from going back to Zanzibar, but in each place he handed over his business to his lieutenants and, of course, collected the ivory due to him. From his attitude it may look as if he had abdicated and accepted European supremacy in Africa. In fact, he was just a little more realistic and diplomatic than his fellow Arabs. Trading had always been his main purpose in life, and with all the cunning resourcefulness at his disposal, he was determined to keep that going as long as he could. In order to maintain a happy balance between continuing his trade and keeping the Europeans happy, he knew he had to co-operate with the Europeans, at least superficially. 'Planting' a few flags and being courteous was not too difficult for him, therefore, and despite his anger, on his way back to the lake he planted Belgian flags and preached patience and diplomacy to the Arabs.

He passed through Mtowa, another L.M.S. station on the west side of Lake Tanganyika, and another Belgian flag was hoisted. He then went on to Ujiji to meet his partner Rumaliza and leave part of the ivory with him. Besides, Rumaliza needed a talking to as he was planning to attack the Belgian post on the lake. 'That fellow Rumaliza listens to no one,' Tippu Tip said.[3] 'I have never seen such an obstinate man as that one.'

Alfred Swann was invited to visit Tippu Tip at Ujiji. He had met him on a previous occasion and found him an engaging personality. 'By far the most important Arab in this drama of Central Africa,' Swann wrote. 'His activity was astonishing. He possessed a frank, manly character, enlivened by humour, and loved immensely to play practical jokes upon his intimate friends. In business there was no beating about the bush: it was always "take it or leave it", and in warfare, "unconditional surrender". His power was sung around most camp-fires, from the East Coast to Stanley Pool on the Congo. His name was sufficient to strike terror into the hearts of all who were liable to attack. (Let me at once place on record my sincere appreciation of the kindness shown to me for many years by both these powerful men (Tippu Tip and Rumaliza), for on one or two occasions they saved my life from the plots of their co-religionists during a period of great disturbance. I cannot say a word for their cruel

[3] Murjebi Family Papers.

trade, but I gratefully, acknowledge their loyal and disinterested attachment to me.'

How disinterested their attachment really was, has often been discussed. The critics of the Rumaliza/Swann friendship said that Rumaliza wanted the English missionary's support in Zanzibar to help him obtain the governorship of the Lake Province; but nobody will ever know for certain. Perhaps Rumaliza and Tippu Tip truly liked Swann as a person. They certainly proved their friendship on more than one occasion, as he says.

It was, therefore, natural for Tippu Tip to invite the English friend to 'tiffin' and to him pour out his bitter complaints against Stanley. As it is, Stanley was not one of Swann's favourite heroes. He considered his latest expedition to rescue Emin Pasha as 'unnecessary and cruel in the extreme ... nothing but shame and guilt can rest on the man who knowingly plunged into the midst of African tribes and poured lead and powder wholesale amongst them, who has caused hundreds of foul murders and left blood, devastation and misery in every footprint and introduced hordes of blood thirsty men headed by the vilest creatures Africa knows, into the "Regions Beyond".' Swann may have exaggerated in his assessment of Stanley and his followers, but the fact remains that he was all ready to listen to Tippu Tip when he arrived in Ujiji.

He found Tippu Tip 'bursting with indignation' at being ordered back to Zanzibar, and showing him the court order, the ex-Governor of the Congo Free State, said: '"Look at this! It is a note ordering me to be at the coast in two months. Stanley accuses me of hindering him on his journey to find Emin Pasha, and alleges that this was the cause of Barttelot's death. If I had wished to stop him, I should not have played with the matter by sending 400 men instead of 600, as per contract; I should have killed him years ago. I do not simply *hinder*, I *destroy*! If I assist, it is at all costs. Who helped Cameron, Speke, Livingstone? Who sent Gleerup from the Congo to Sweden? Who saved your life, and those of all your party; was it not me? Have I attempted to hinder any missionaries, although they are not of my religion and hate my business of catching slaves? Tell me! Is there a single European traveller who can honestly say I was not his friend?"' Swann agreed with him, but Tippu Tip could not be stopped, he was in a raging temper. '"I am mad with anger when I think of what we did for Stanley during his first and second journey through this country. In order to make a big work out of nothing, he went up the Congo to find Emin Pasha; why not have walked up the much less expensive road from the East Coast? He came to Zanzibar and begged me to go round the Cape with him, and to bring my people, all expenses to be paid by himself. I did not desire to go, choosing rather to walk, as I have always done, and to transact business as I passed my various depots; but he would take no denial, so, out of courtesy, I accompanied him. He needed my assistance to obtain porters, and, because only 200 out of 600 men I sent ran away, I am accused of wanting to hinder him. Do they not desert from all Europeans, as well as from Arabs? The truth is your countrymen are criticising his work and the loss of Barttelot, and he is wanting to blame me. Barttelot lost his life through bad temper; it was entirely his own fault. I was hundreds of miles distant, and lost money through the cannibal porters running away. I cannot understand Stanley. Without my help he could never have gone down the Congo; and no sooner did he reach Europe, than he claimed all my country. Surely your people must be unjust!"'

Swann assured Tippu Tip that European law was just, and advised him to go and tell his story in Zanzibar. 'They will listen to you,' he said, 'for we are accustomed to weigh both sides of a question and love justice.'

Instead of soothing his angry host, Swann was getting deeper and deeper into an argument he would have preferred to avoid. 'Do you?' Tippu Tip promptly retorted. 'Then how did you get India?'

'We fought for it,' Swann replied.

'Then what you fight for, and win, belongs to you by right of conquest?'

'Yes, that is European law.'

'So it is with us Arabs,' Tippu Tip added with satisfaction. 'Have we ever tried to rob you of India?'

'I may ask you, in reply, do these pagans try to rob you of Ujiji? The jackal cannot rob the lion,' Swann bravely went on. Somehow Tippu Tip skirted around this question.

'Very well, then. I came here as a young man, fought these natives and subdued them, losing both friends and treasure in the struggle. Is it not therefore mine by both your law and ours?'

'It is only yours so long as you govern and use it properly.'

'And who is to be my judge?'

'Europe.'

135

'Aha! Now you speak the truth. Do not let us talk of justice; people are only just when it pays. The white man is stronger than I am; they will eat my possessions as I ate those of the pagans, and ...' he paused.

'And what?' Swann insisted.

'Some one will eat up yours. I see clouds in the sky! The thunder is near. I am going.'

This conversation took place in 1890 and Swann says he was listening to the capitulation of the greatest man-hunter of Central Africa. He was listening to an accurate prediction of the Europeans' future in Africa and India.

Still believing *any* white man's word carried great weight, Tippu Tip added: 'Tell Europe Stanley lies; and tell them also, if they love justice, as you say, to compensate me for stealing my country.'

Swann had been listening patiently, and partly agreeing with the 'great man', but as a Christian missionary he must have felt that a little preaching was necessary at this point and when Tippu Tip asked, 'Have you nothing to say to my arguments?', he said:

'Yes, I have! I know you are strong and wise enough to hear it without being angry with me. Europe has sickened of your cruel slave operations, and determined to stop them. That's the cloud you see in the sky, from which the rain is already falling at the coast!' At this point Swann gives the conversation a more dramatic tone. Tippu Tip's 'long lean sword lay on the couch by his side, and this terrible man-hunter could have cut down the ambassador of freedom, at any moment.' But he didn't. Tippu Tip was indulging in one of his favourite pastimes: arguing with a man who was probably better educated academically, but in practice a simple Victorian missionary. Tippu Tip was having a wonderful game, and at the same time he was enlisting a sympathetic ear, an English ear, to help him fight British law and Stanley.

'It seems to me,' Tippu Tip went on, 'that Europe does not like something I do, and therefore is determined to ruin me. Is that it?'

'Yes, if you do not abandon your trade.'

'You Europeans do many things I abominate, such as eating swine's flesh; but you never saw an Arab try to destroy your farmyards on account of his aversion to your practices.'

'No, I have not. But there is a vast difference between pigs and men, and, if you will permit me, I will ask you some questions.'

Being given leave to ask anything he wanted, Swann proceeded to go into the 'who-made-men question', but first of all he had to find out if Hamed bin Muhammed el Murjebi, alias Tippu Tip, believed in one God, which landed the missionary into a little bit of trouble as the answer was, yes, he did, but the Christians said there were three. Swann doesn't go into the details of his own answer to the Christian meaning of Trinity. It was enough for Swann to have Tippu Tip's confirmation of his firm belief that God created all men, including pagans, which left the slave hunter open to a Christian lecture.

'And yet every day you deliberately destroy His good work, catching and killing slaves!' Swann declaimed. 'Has God made a mistake by creating them, and asked you to rectify His error?'

'They would not acknowledge Him, and therefore have forfeited His protection,' said the staunch Mohammedan.

'Then if your son becomes undutiful to you, does it give me licence to blow out his brains? Is that Arab justice?'

'Abraham, Isaac and Jacob made many slaves, and God did not punish them,' was Tippu Tip's final reply, making it quite clear that he'd had enough of the lecture.

'This face-to-face encounter,' Swann wrote, 'eight hundred miles from British protection, was fascinating. Wealth, power, intelligence, ambition, and cruelty sat represented in that one figure on the sofa. Thousands of men and guns were at that moment at his command, but his active brain had weighed them in the balance against yonder little rain-cloud, and found them wanting.'

Tippu Tip left Ujiji and his vast empire behind and never saw them again. Swann remained a good friend and often visited him in Zanzibar, but despite Tippu Tip's advice; Rumaliza and the other Arabs stayed behind, and without Tippu Tip's restraining influence, they fought the Belgians until they were totally destroyed.

CHAPTER SIXTEEN

The End of the Hunt

Thirty years of hunting for ivory and slaves had come to an end for Tippu Tip, and his return journey to the coast in March 1890, was a sad one. No honours or hero's welcome would be awaiting him at the end of the long journey, he knew, and as he walked towards his father's and grandfather's stronghold near Tabora, he was not surprised to come across the full evidence of German colonial power.

Herr von Bülow now governed at Urambo, where Mirambo's son had taken over after his father's death in 1884. Tippu Tip had no wish to meet the German Governor, but the local English missionary advised the slaver to pay a courtesy visit, and Tippu Tip was surprised to be treated with great deference by the German who later asked to travel to the coast with him. Even in 1890 it was safer to travel with Tippu Tip, than with German trained askaris.

He continued his march and reached Tabora just after Emin Pasha, now Imperial Commissioner, had passed through on a tour of inspection of his new province. He had left a letter for Tippu Tip reassuring him that Stanley's charges 'were false'. He had also left evidence of his methods of administration. On the Commissioner's orders a number of Arabs had been executed and the German flag had been firmly 'planted'.

From Tabora Emin Pasha had sent a German flag to Rumaliza with orders to hoist it in Ujiji, whilst he himself had gone on to other districts to establish German law and order, hanging a few more rebellious Arabs on the way. His activities never allowed him to reach Ujiji to enforce the 'flag-planting' orders. In October 1892 he was murdered near Manyema, one of Tippu Tip's main strongholds, at the instigation of the local Arab slave traders.

'Emin Pasha was a Mohammedan. He prayed in our mosques, and he betrayed our faith,' Rumaliza explained to Alfred Swann showing him the German flag the Pasha had sent him. 'He sent that flag to replace our own, and then went to Nyanza and hanged several Arabs in cold blood; therefore the Arabs swore to take his life. If he had come this way it would have been the same. Instead of which he tried to escape down the Congo.'

Rumaliza had not taken part in the actual murder of Emin Pasha, but like all the other Arabs, he was completely committed, incensed and ready to fight. Arab opposition to European expansion had been surprisingly slow, but now that Tippu Tip was out of the way, and they had no hope of assistance from Zanzibar, the Arabs were determined to fight for survival however desperate and hopeless the outcome might be.

Sultan Barghash had given up his claims on the mainland since the German blockade of 1885 and when in 1886 the German and British Governments started negotiations for their respective 'Spheres of Influence',[1] the Arabs had set fire to the Belgian station at Stanley Falls. That marked the beginning of hostilities between Arabs and Europeans, and although Tippu Tip was a controlling influence during his period as Governor of the Congo Free State, more and more disturbances broke out. Arabs and Africans resisted the Germans in various parts of Tanganyika and the Belgians in the Upper Congo, and by 1892 the situation had become explosive. It all ended in 1894 with disastrous results for the Arabs.

That was four years after Tippu Tip's visit to Tabora on his way back to Zanzibar, but in 1890 when he reached Tabora the Arabs still believed in their ability to stop the European occupation, especially if Tippu Tip sided with them. 'Stay with us, we will protect you,' they said to him.[2] 'Together we will fight the Europeans. In Zanzibar they will put you in jail or even hang you.'

'How is it that you think you can hold me if the Europeans want me?' he asked the Arabs promising him asylum. 'All of you

[1] Ever since the reign of Sultan Said, the Arabs had been pressing to be taken under British protection, offering concessions etc., but the British Government was completely opposed to any type of colonial involvement with Africa. This attitude changed completely as soon as the Germans acquired land in Tanganyika.

[2] Murjebi Family Papers.

have gone mad. How can you protect *me* when Emin Pasha has just killed several people, yet you did nothing. You are crazy, I am leaving.'

But he didn't. Severe dysentery and malaria kept him in Tabora for six more months. For the first two months his life was in the balance, but he was taken good care of by the Catholic White Fathers and his step-mother Nyaso. Nyaso had fully accepted the German take-over of Tabora and was doing brisk business supplying porters for the frequent caravans.

As soon as he was able to move Tippu Tip left Tabora despite the fact that nobody expected him to survive the journey. He was so weak that for the first time in his life he had to be carried in a litter. He expected nothing but trouble when he reached the coast, and yet he forced his caravan to march as fast as possible.

The swaying and bumping of the litter made him restless and irritable, and he soon gave it up for a mule. 'I felt like a helpless old man, being carried as I was between two of my slaves,' he said.[3] 'And although I had never submitted to riding a mule before, I decided it was better than riding between two men.' It was also more dignified for his entry into Mpwapwa. Up until then he had always said, 'I am a poor Arab whom Allah has raised to greatness. I walk so that I will not forget my humble origin.'

Mpwapwa was a very important centre between the coast and Tabora in the days of the great caravans. The Church Missionary Society had chosen it as one of their first stations in 1876 and now the German administration was well entrenched there.

Tippu Tip had an agent at Mpwapwa, but the first people he saw there were the missionaries who informed him that Lieutenant Jameson's brother and his widow had arrived and were anxious to speak to him about a story that Stanley had brought back to Europe. According to Stanley Jameson had bought a woman slave and then given her to his Manyema porters and watched them devour her in Tippu Tip's presence.

At the mention of Stanley's name and his intrigues Tippu Tip burst into a long and furious attack on the explorer. The man was nothing but a publicity-seeking liar, according to Tippu Tip. 'He tried to make me responsible for his failures when he went to look for Emin Pasha, he tried to smear Major Barttelot's character, and now Jameson. I am very sorry,' he said to Jame-

[3] Murjebi Family Papers.

son's widow and his brother. [4] 'Stanley fabricated many stories to remove Europe's attention from his own failures. I always knew him to be a liar, but sometimes it is difficult to know when he is lying. As when he promised to cover me in presents and money after the Congo trip and all he sent me was a photograph. Then when I went on the last trip with him, he gave me a miserable little puppy dog on the boat to the Cape, and I immediately passed it on to Jameson. I never saw Jameson or any other European do anything like what Stanley says. He is a liar.'

Recovered in health and ready for battle with Stanley, he reached Bagamoyo where he conferred with Herr Schmidt, the German Administrator who seems to have treated him rather well considering that the Germans were busy hanging Arab slave traders wherever they could catch them. In fact, both the Germans on the coast and the British Consul in Zanzibar treated him with the 'utmost kindness', he says.

On various occasions he was asked about Jameson but he continued to defend the young officer's integrity of character and to curse Stanley. He was never asked to answer Stanley's charges against himself. For some unknown reason, Stanley had withdrawn all charges against Tippu Tip and a document was signed by the slaver and Stanley's representatives, Smith, Mackenzie & Co. 'Stanley's charges and his lies were finished with,' Tippu Tip remarked with satisfaction. [4]

There was nothing left for Tippu Tip to do now but retire gracefully. A very hard situation to accept for a man in his middle fifties and still full of life and ambition; but he had no illusions left about his Congo empire and even less now that he was back in Zanzibar. He knew the Congo was doomed for the Arabs and it was only a question of time before the whole set up collapsed for the slavers and traders. A few pockets of Arab and African resistance would still give the Germans trouble in Tanganyika, and the Congo Arabs were about to embark on their last desperate effort against the Belgians, but Tippu Tip knew that it couldn't last very long and he had no intention of going back to the Congo to take part in the last fight, even if he had been allowed to go back.

Not so his son Sef and his partner Rumaliza. They both remained behind to the end. Whilst Rumaliza concentrated on harassing the Belgians on Lake Tanganyika and the Germans

[4] Murjebi Family Papers, and Brode's *Tippu Tip.*

east of Ujiji; Sef went back to Kasongo and took over the leadership of his father's old territories. Unfortunately for Sef, the chief of that region, Lutete, who for years acknowledged Tippu Tip as his master, and had become one of his most loyal subjects, now made an agreement with the Belgians. Unaware of this alliance, Sef tried to impose his authority on Lutete and was forced to retreat to Nyangwe, but not before a rumour of his death reached the Nyangwe Arabs who immediately took revenge and murdered two Belgians. The fight was now on in earnest. The Africans, realising that the Belgians were now in a stronger position than their former masters, sided with the Belgians providing them with boats to cross over to Nyangwe and the Arabs were defeated. News of the Nyangwe disaster reached the remaining Arabs at Kasongo and they in turn murdered two Europeans. Dhannis, the Belgian commander, then marched on Kasongo and there defeated the Arabs with Lutete's help. It was at this time that Emin Pasha was murdered by the Arabs at Manyema and his stocks of ivory (3 tons), rifles and ammunition went to his attackers who were beginning to run short of arms. His diary was part of the booty, but was later recovered and eventually published in Germany.

There was fighting everywhere from Lake Nyasa to the Congo Basin. The Congo Arabs retreated to Stanley Falls and were defeated again. Those who escaped, including Sef, joined Rumaliza on Lake Tanganyika and from there carried on the fight.

Throughout these disturbances Rumaliza behaved in his usual 'gentlemanly fashion' towards the L.M.S., and his friend Swann wrote that although for a whole year the missions were completely cut off from the East coast, they were never molested. The missionaries once managed to get a message through to the coast by writing in Pitman's shorthand backwards, to make it look like Arabic. The message, rolled inside the barrel of a musket, got through the German lines despite the fact that, as Swann says, 'the Imperial Eagle had fixed its talons on the quarry and did not relax its hold until it had brought about its utter destruction'.

Among the last to surrender to the Germans were the Ruga-Ruga and the Wagogo. Despite the fact that their great leader Mirambo had been dead for over ten years and his son had virtually no power over them, the bandits and their neighbours the Wagogo, were not prepared to give up their traditional demand for hongo from all travellers. On one occasion a German officer was ordered to make camp by the Wagogo until he paid hongo. The officer camped but all the Wagogo received was a lot of lead and fire. They never asked for hongo again.

The last battle between the Arabs and the Belgians was fought on October 20th, 1893 on the River Luama, west of Lake Tanganyika. It was a bloody fight and both Belgians and Arabs lost a great number of men, but the Arabs were completely defeated and Tippu Tip's son, Sef, was one of the casualties. His had been a short and violent life, having never achieved the ability for statesmanship and diplomacy which were his father's natural gifts.

Tippu Tip's losses through the defeat of the Arabs were immense. Professor Brode wrote that the ex 'Uncrowned King' had lost 157,000 lbs. of ivory, 42,000 lbs. of supplies, 20,000 muskets and tons of ammunition. Many of his relations had died in the fighting, but Sef was the greatest loss of all. He could not forgive himself for the fact that he had allowed his eldest and beloved son to remain behind and be killed.

Somehow, his partner Rumaliza survived the battle and the complete collapse of his world. One day he turned up in Zanzibar aboard a small fishing dhow and immediately went to his friend Tippu Tip. The meeting was not a happy one. In fact it was the beginning of a long and nasty fight over money.

Despite his great losses in the Congo, Tippu Tip did not appear to be exactly penniless. He still owned large properties both in Zanzibar and along the mainland coast. Some of the time he lived in a very comfortable house in Zanzibar (which was turned into a hotel after his death), and some of the time in one of his country houses, surrounded by his wives, concubines, fourteen children, their wives and concubines, numerous grandchildren and, of course, slaves. 'He had hundreds of acres of land worked by his slaves,' one of his daughters-in-law said many years later. 'The slaves worked in the morning for him and then in the afternoon did whatever they pleased. They could till their fields which he had given them or, if they wanted to work on his estates, they were paid for it. The lucky ones were the household slaves. We had hundreds of them, mostly just for show, and their main duty was to wear lovely clothes and look impressive. After he died, hundreds of his slaves became free. They had a good life with Tippu Tip, but they became beggars once they became free men. A lot of the women from his harem became water-

143

carriers. Nothing. In the harem they were like ladies, but when they became free they were just water-carriers. A lot of them became prostitutes.'[5]

She goes on to describe her own marriage to one of Tippu Tip's sons. Tippu Tip had arranged for the marriage between his son and the fourteen year old daughter of a 'respectable' family living on Pemba island. The bride arrived in Zanzibar on a special dhow, painted in bright colours, heavily carved and festooned with flags and streamers. The bride, dressed in silks and brocades, reclined on Persian carpets surrounded by her women slaves. As the bridal dhow approached Zanzibar, Tippu Tip's boats went out to meet it. They were also brightly painted and covered in buntings. The slaves who manned the boats were dressed in red and gold embroidered gowns.

'Of course, the slaves waited on us,' she goes on reminiscing. 'We women never lifted a hand. Anything we wanted was instantly brought to us by the slaves. My father-in-law, Tippu Tip was a marvellous man. His son, my husband, not the one who was killed in the Congo, one of the other sons, he was never the man his father was. He was a typical son of a rich father, but everybody worshipped his father, Tippu Tip. All the Arabs were generous, but none as generous as he. Every day, forty or fifty poor people would come to our house for food and they were never turned away empty. At a certain hour the slaves would blow a horn as a signal and within ten minutes the courtyard would be full of people. At the end of Ramadan, Tippu Tip provided all the poor in Zanzibar with new clothes.'

Not exactly a picture to impress the survivor of the Congo disaster. Rumaliza had always been jealous of Tippu Tip's success, not only as a wealthy trader, but as a leader of men and the widely acknowledged 'great' among the Arabs. Not only acknowledged by the Africans and the Arabs, but by all the Europeans who had dealings with him. After all, what did Rumaliza's friendship with the missionary Swann mean in comparison with Livingstone, Stanley, Cameron and a host of others. Even now in Zanzibar and on the mainland, where all the ex slavers were very much *persona non grata* to both the British and the Germans, Tippu Tip managed to maintain an honoured position. He was

[5] The number of brothels grew to an alarming number after the first rush for 'emancipation papers' and it was even reported by the British Consul to the Foreign Office as an evil by-product of freedom.

144

still considered an authority on matters of state by the Sultan and the British representatives, and his advice was often sought and heeded.

A British Consul, Sir Charles Eliot, became a good friend of the ex slaver, and not only enjoyed his company, but greatly admired him. 'His features were of the negro type,' Sir Charles wrote, [6] 'and produced at first an impression that he was a low-caste hybrid; but this impression was dispelled by his polite and dignified manners and his flow of speech. The tremulous twitching of his eyelids was very noticeable, and it was generally believed that this was the origin of his name Tippoo Tib, "the blinker", although he himself, not liking the personal allusion, had other explanations. The touch of mockery in his manner and language, was very noticeable, but not unpleasant nor discourteous. He did not live to execute the journey to Europe which he was planning; but not long ago, in the language of Mohammedanism, he removed to "the abode of permanency", though some Hindu cycle of transmigration would seem more congenial to such a wanderer and explorer.'

Rumaliza, therefore, decided that his ex partner could well afford to share some of his accumulated wealth, but Tippu Tip was far from willing to share anything with a man who had swindled him on more than one occasion.

Since the day they first met in Ujiji in 1881, Rumaliza had often borrowed and never returned anything. On one occasion Tippu Tip had left him in Tabora with 80,000 dollars' worth of goods to be sent on to Ujiji. The goods never arrived as Rumaliza had managed to squander most of these on trading of his own, Tippu Tip claims. In fact, according to him, anything Rumaliza ever handled for his partner ended up by 'falling into the big hole of Lake Tanganyika', Tippu Tip said. To add insult to injury, Rumaliza picked a quarrel with Nyaso, 'although he knew she was my step-mother'. The resourceful old woman was doing business with the Europeans and Rumaliza objected strongly. Co-operation with the Europeans had long been a bone of contention between the two Arabs, and Tippu Tip had often called Rumaliza a fool for not following his example.

Rumaliza had more against Tippu Tip than his infatuation with the Europeans. Tippu Tip was rich and Rumaliza had lost almost everything, therefore he brought a case against his former

[6] Sir Charles Eliot, *The East African Protectorate*, 1905.

partner demanding a quarter of everything Tippu Tip had. The case was tried in Dar es Salaam and it stretched on for months with both parties accusing the other of endless misdeeds. Rumaliza produced a document signed by Tippu Tip and Bwana Nzige stating that he was entitled to a quarter of all Tippu Tip's profits, and although Tippu Tip and his cousin Bwana Nzige claimed the document was a forgery, the court awarded Rumaliza all of Tippu Tip's property on the mainland coast and 6,000 dollars.

Tippu Tip was furious, and in his biography he says that Rumaliza was lucky the authorities didn't know about his deeds on Lake Tanganyika and Tabora where he was a party to the murder of Europeans and fomented various revolts against the Belgians and the Germans. 'He was responsible for all the troubles,' he said. [7] 'But he was lucky, nobody had seen, and all he got was a bullet in a finger.' Nevertheless, Tippu Tip lived to see justice done. Rumaliza once again lost everything through lawyers and court expenses, and Tippu Tip ends up by saying: 'Mali ya harumu yanakwenda njia ya haramu.' Ill gotten gains never prosper. [7]

The outcome of the law suit left him resentful and disappointed in human nature, but not exactly poor. He went on living in Zanzibar in the ease that his daughter-in-law so well described and very much enjoying his new position as unofficial adviser to each succeeding Sultan.

For the first time in his life he was able to enjoy his family and the fruits of his long years in the interior. He had never had time to enjoy his children, but now dozens of grandchildren sat around him in the gardens of his town-house, [8] listening to their grandfather's fantastic stories of adventure; or walking with him in the grounds of his country estate where the whole family moved to during the hot months. This was in the autumn and it was the big event of the year for the family. Great excitement always preceded the move.

'On the day of departure everyone was up before dawn,' his daughter-in-law said. 'We women rode snow-white mules, with saddles studded with gold and silver. A slave would kneel and you stepped on his back to mount. Of course, we were all veiled in those days and wore our long robes. A slave walked by each

[7] Brode's *Tippu Tip*.
[8] Until quite recently the house still bore his name.

of us holding a parasol over our heads and other slaves, on Arabian horses and armed with muskets inlaid with silver, rode on either side as a guard—just for show, of course. Everything was carried on the heads of slaves and we had a line of two or three hundred of them. There was an old slave who acted as major-domo and sometimes we girls would race each other on our donkeys and get ahead of the main party which always made the old fellow furious with us. A party under another old slave had gone on to the country estate several days before, so when we arrived everything was ready for us. We amused ourselves walking under the big mango and fig trees—they've been cut down now to make room for the clove plantation—or playing with our pet animals or using the baths. Mostly we just sat around and gossiped.

'Tippu Tip was always very courteous to the women but he didn't talk to us much. In those days, when an Arab went to see a woman, it was for a purpose and there wasn't much conversation involved. He was always most correct in his behaviour. He only had one wife by then, although our religion allows four, and he made a point of spending the morning with her. The afternoon he spent with his favourite concubines. Then in the evening he saw the other concubines too.' He was by then in his late sixties and often suffered from bouts of malaria and dysentery, but women never ceased to please him.

Just before Tippu Tip returned to Zanzibar, an agreement had been signed between Britain and Germany, and by the 4th of November, 1890, the future of East Africa was settled. Germany, having paid the Sultan of Zanzibar £200,000 for the coastal strip, now owned the whole area later known as Tanganyika. Kenya and Uganda became the British East Africa Protectorate, and the British Protectorate of Zanzibar was also proclaimed. The slave trade, the backbone of all Zanzibar's wealth, had supposedly become an historical fact by then.

The last known case of a slave-dhow in East African waters was reported in 1899. Twenty-three years after Sultan Barghash had issued a proclamation prohibiting slave caravans approaching the coast from the interior. Even the domestic slaves could now apply to the courts for their freedom, but although at the beginning of this new law they applied in thousands, by 1905 only a trickle came forth to receive their 'Emancipation Papers'. They had seen what happened to the slaves who were no longer the responsibility of a master. 'Who will look after me when I am sick and too old to work?' they asked. [9]

In his lifetime Tippu Tip had seen many changes. He had started trading at the peak of the slave trade era, and he died at the end of it. At least the official end of it. According to the Anti-Slavery Society's annual reports, a form of slavery is still practised in the Arab world, and slavery of one kind or another will always be practised; but at the time of Tippu Tip's death, the slave caravans, the markets, the raids and the middle passage, were already a thing of the past.

Hamed bin Muhammed bin Juma Rajad el Murjebi, Tippu Tip to friend and foe, died in his Zanzibar house on the 13th June, 1905. Malaria the plague of all who travelled in Africa in those days, finally killed him when he was about seventy years old.

Alfred Swann must have expressed the opinion of many who knew Tippu Tip, when he referred to a small announcement which appeared in *The Times*. That newspaper simply announced the death 'of that notorious slaver', but said nothing of the slaver's other activities, and Swann suggests that the editors could have been a little more generous by mentioning what 'some of our great geographical societies in Europe had acknowledged. How much they were indebted to Tip-pu-Tib for allowing explorers to travel where he was in power, collecting valuable scientific data.' Or, as a French traveller, Captain Trivier later wrote, they could at least have mentioned him as the Arab 'Cooks' for white travellers in Africa.

Tippu Tip himself would not have been pleased with the announcement in *The Times*. The ingratitude of Europeans always upset him, but as he said to Swann, 'Justice will be done. The Europeans are throwing the Arabs out now, but they will be thrown out in turn.'

He left a fortune of £50,000 invested in property, but his heirs were so many that none of them lived as Tippu Tip had lived.

With him an era of adventure, exploration and discoveries had come to an end. Great changes were taking place. Some were good and some not so good for the people of Africa, but at least one recognisable good change was the end of the trade in human beings.

[9] *Zanzibar Reports*, 1870-1905.

Most of the explorers Tippu Tip had known had died. Even his arch-enemy, Henry Morton Stanley, had died the year before.

Professor Heinrich Brode, the biographer who had known him in the days of his retirement wrote: 'The paths travelled out by his blood-stained hands have supplied the framework for all the subsequent cartography of German East Africa and the Congo Free State. Thus a life-work of destruction has served to aid the advance of civilization.'

'Kila Mlango na Nfunguo Wakwe'
'Every Door Has its Key'
SWAHILI PROVERB

Historical and Genealogical Background to Tippu Tip's Life and Times

The Arabs have traded along the East African coast from time immemorial. Before the advent of the steam engine, the trade-winds or *monsoons* were the most important factor of this traffic between the Asian and African coasts bordering the Indian Ocean. From November to March the hot north-east monsoon blows down the East African coast from Asia and with the monsoon came the Ocean-going dhows from Aden, Hadhramant, Muscat in the Persian Gulf and India. At the end of March the wind turns and the south-west monsoon carried the heavily laden dhows back to their native ports. Not only Arabs, but Persians and Indians were certain of a safe return home with the spring monsoon after trading on the East African coast during the winter months. This annual trading was a regular practice; the Arabian dhows came laden with goods which were used for barter, and went back loaded with ivory, gum-copal, [1] spices, grain *and* slaves.

The beautiful dhows still sail before the *Kazkazi* [2] and as they proudly lie at anchor by the old ports of Mombasa, Lamu, Dar es Salaam or Zanzibar, one cannot help but admire these ancient sailing ships which have defied time and technology. Except for the nature of their cargo, they sail today as they always did.

There is historical evidence of this trading recorded by ancient travellers. In the *Periplus of the Erythraean Sea,* as the Greeks named the Indian Ocean, a Greek merchant-seaman, about A.D.

[1] A hard resin used for lacquers and polishes.
[2] Monsoon.

80, wrote:.... 'the people of Muza (Mocha), now hold it (the East African coast) under authority, and send thither many large ships, using Arab captains and agents who are familiar with the natives and intermarry with them and who know the whole coast and understand the language. They imported lances, hatchets, daggers, awls and glass and at some places a little wine and wheat, not for trade, but to serve for getting the goodwill of the savages. They trade for ivory in great quantities, rhinoceros-horn, tortoise-shell and palm-oil.' And from the coast near Ras Hafun (100 miles south of Cape Guardafui), 'slaves of the better sort which are brought to Egypt in increasing numbers.'

That particular market had been exhausted, or at least it was no longer profitable, long before Tippu Tip's time. In the 19th century the regions west and south-west of Zanzibar provided the thousands of slaves needed for the Asian markets and the dominions of the Sultan of Zanzibar.

After the Greeks we have records from Arab sources. Their chronicles and narratives, ruined towns, coins and pottery have come to light all along the East African coast to give evidence of the steady traffic between Africa and Asia. Even Marco Polo in his *Travels* mentions that the great Kubla Khan had sent messengers to Madagascar, 'on the pretext of demanding the release of one of his servants who had been detained there but in reality to examine into the circumstances of the country'. Early Chinese books make frequent reference to the Zinj coast, as the East African coast was then known, but it was not until the Ming Dynasty that the Chinese actually visited East Africa. Again Marco Polo says:.... 'There are many savages with bodies as black as lacquer and with frizzled hair. They are enticed by food, then caught and carried off for slaves to the Ta'shi (Arab) countries where they fetch a high price. They are used for gate-keepers. It is said they do not long for their kinsfolk....'

After the Prophet's death in A.D. 632, the main body of the Arabs fought for Islam through Persia, Syria, Egypt, North Africa and finally as far as the Pyrenees; but the Omani Arabs had no part in these religious wars, they were fighting among themselves. About A.D. 695, a faction under chiefs Suleiman and Said rose against the Caliph, and having lost the fight, fled to the Land of Zinji and settled there. There were other Arabs who took refuge on the coast of East Africa and the islands opposite the coast. About A.D. 920 the 'Seven brothers of El Hasa', again escaping persecution at home, founded Mogadishu and Barawa, and in the same century 'Hassan-bin-Ali and his six sons' sailed in seven ships and founded six different settlements—or so Arab legend has it. Hassan, the father, founded Kilwa, the sons founded Mombasa, Pemba and Johanna in the Comoro Islands. There is no record of the other three settlements or sons, but the Arab chroniclers are not known for accuracy. The famous Arab *Chronicles of Kilwa* are a mixture of history and romance. Had these chronicles been more accurate, the geography of East Africa would have been recorded long before the advent of the European explorers.

Little is known of the Arabs on the coast during the Middle Ages. Apart from the *Chronicles of Kilwa* and the *Swahili History of Pate*, a few writings exist giving names and successions of the ruling sheikhs and sultans. More detailed were works by Arabs living outside East Africa. For instance, books by travellers such as Masudi of Baghdad in the 10th century, the map drawn and annotated by the Arab Idrisi in the 12th century, Yaqut the Greek freedman in the 13th century, and Ibn Battuta of Tangier in the 14th century. From all these works and more recent excavations, it is evident that by the 15th century the Arab and Persian settlements were Mogadishu, Barawa, Siu, Pate, Lamu, Malindi, Kilifi, Mombasa, Vumba, Pemba, Zanzibar, Mafia, Kilwa, Mozambique and Sofala.

The fact that Arab influence stopped just south of Sofala, was no doubt due to the monsoon which turns at that point. Most of the settlements were on islands, some like Zanzibar, a fair distance from the mainland, and some like Mombasa, Kilwa, Pate, Siu and Lamu, separated by a small strip of sea from the coast. They were all strategic points for the exploitation of the mainland, and by the 15th century there were at least thirty-seven towns between Kilwa and Mogadishu.

By the beginning of the 16th century when the Portuguese conquered the coast from Sofala to Mogadishu, they found that the Arab towns were strongly fortified and properly planned. The houses were mostly built of stone or coral and mortar, with large windows, inner gardens and courts. Heavily carved doors and frames adorned the entrances, and the mosques had beautiful examples of Persian art.

The Arabs, therefore, had been maintaining their traditional way of life, including the eternal quarrelling among themselves, which proved fatal to them when within a period of a few years the Portuguese took their towns one by one. As they themselves were not united, they never achieved any sort of unity in their colonial dominions. The closest they came to this unity was in the 19th century when Seyyid Said moved his court from Muscat to Zanzibar. Before that period each town and its surrounding region, fought its neighbour for supremacy, the fortunes of one or the other going up or down following each squabble. Mombasa and Malindi were always at each other's walls, and Kilwa held sway for decades. The various African chiefs sometimes sided with one or the other contestant, and regularly fought them both. The Arab settlements were often fighting off the surrounding tribes, and they fought the Portuguese throughout their occupation which lasted on and off until the middle of the 18th century. The defeat of the Portuguese was only due to a temporary unification of the Omani Arabs, but on this occasion they were united long enough to repulse the Portuguese as far as the Ravuma River where they have remained ever since.

The society which prospered along this Arab coastal strip and on the islands, was not purely Arab. Closely associated, but not of the ruling class, were the Indians, whose involvement with the African coast was almost as old as the Arabs'. They were then, as until recently, the money lenders, the bankers, the importers and the retail traders. A lot of the shipping was owned by the Indians, and as the Arabs never quite developed the Indian acumen for money, the latter were indispensable to the prosperity of these settlements. Each succeeding Sultan entrusted his treasury and the collecting of customs' dues and taxes to Indians. The famous Indian banker, Taria Topan, financed most of Tippu Tip's caravans and was a very important man in the economy of Zanzibar during the reign of three Sultans.

Another very important group was the ever-increasing half-caste population, now known as the Wa-Swahili.[3] Their status varied according to the degree of Arab blood in their family tree.

In Tippu Tip's case the African blood which left such strong negroid features in him, went back four generations, when his great-great-grandfather married an African woman.

Tippu Tip's great-great-grandfather, Juma bin Muhammed el

[3] Swahili meaning 'Coast People' from the Arabic word *sahil* or coast.

Nebhani, was a member of a Muscat family who came to the East African coast at the end of the 18th century. He settled in Mbwa Maji, a village south of present-day Dar es Salaam, where he married a local woman. From her he had three children. One son, Mohammed; and two daughters, one of whom was named Mwana Arabu,[4] Tippu Tip's great-grandmother.

Old Juma went back to Muscat towards the end of his life, and with him went his son Mohammed. The African wife and his two daughters were left behind. The son later came back to East Africa, bringing with him a friend by the name of Rajad bin Muhammed bin Said el Murjebi. Rajad married Mohammed's sister Mwana, and from their union came Juma bin Rajad, Tippu Tip's grandfather, who made a great name for himself as a leader of caravans; his influence extending as far as Lake Tanganyika. The grandfather of the dreaded warlord Mirambo[5] of Unyamwezi, was appointed chief of Ugoa with Juma's support. This family alliance later proved very helpful to Tippu Tip when his caravans had to cross the territory Mirambo terrorised and controlled.

Juma's son, Tippu Tip's father, Muhammed bin Juma, who in turn established himself as a caravan leader and trader in the Unyamwezi region (Tabora), took as first wife Chief Fundikira's[6] daughter, Karunde. Apart from a large number of local concubines, most of the Arabs living in the interior married some powerful chief's daughter to ensure the stability of their trading in the region where they operated. Tippu Tip's father was no exception, but for him marriage to Karunde, daughter of a great chief, was not simply a marriage of convenience. He was very fond of her and was always ready to fight any enemy of her family. He was also a good Mohammedan, therefore back in Zanzibar he married the daughter of a good Muscat family, Bint Habib bin Bushir, Tippu Tip's mother. He hardly ever saw Bint Habib as he lived mostly in Tabora, but so long as the 'pure Arab' lineage was assured, nobody seemed to mind.

---

[4] Meaning Arab child.
[5] Mirambo, 1830-1884.
[6] Fundikira, sometimes spelt Fundi Kira. The family still exists.

Bibliography

Buxton, T. F. *The African Slave Trade & Its Remedy*, 1839/1840

Baker, Sir Samuel. *Ismailia*, 1874; *Albert Nyanza, Great Basin of the Nile*, 1866

Brode, Heinrich. *Tippu Tip*, 1903

Barnard, F. L. 'Three Years Cruise in the Mozambique Channel', 1848

Burton, Sir Richard. *First Footsteps in East Africa*, 1856; *The Lake Regions of Central Africa*, 1860; *The Lands of Cazembe*, 1873; *Zanzibar: City, Island and Coast*, 1872

Barttelot, W. G. *The Life of Edmund Musgrave Barttelot*, 1890

Boteler, T. *Narrative of a Voyage of Discovery to Africa and Arabia, Performed in His Majesty's Ships Leven and Barracouta, from 1821 to 1826, Under the Command of Capt. F. W. Owen, R.N.*, 1835

Coupland, Sir Reginald. *Wilberforce*, 1923; *Kirk of the Zambesi*, 1928; *East Africa & Its Invaders*, 1938; *The Exploitation of East Africa*, 1939

Casati, Gaetano. *Ten Years in Equatoria & the Return with Emin Pasha*, 1891

Christie, J. *Cholera Epidemics in East Africa*, 1876

Cameron, V. Lovett. *Across Africa*, 1877

Comber, Thomas. *Missionary Pioneer to the Congo*

Colomb, Capt. R.N. *Slave Catching in the Indian Ocean*, 1873

Dawson, E. C. *James Hannington, First Bishop of Eastern Equatorial Africa*, 1887

Devereux, W. C. *A Cruise in the Gordon*, 1869

Eliot, Sir Charles. *The East African Protectorate*, 1905

Equiano, Olandah. *The Interesting Narrative of the Life of, or Gustavus Vassa, the African Slave*, 1789

Fitzgerald, W. W. A. *Travels in British East Africa, Zanzibar and Pemba*, 1898

Hamilton, Genesta. *Princes of Zinj*, 1957

Hinde, Sidney L. *The Fall of the Congo Arabs*, 1897

Ingram, W. H. *Zanzibar, It's History and It's People*

Johnston, Sir Harry. *The Congo River*, 1884; *The Nile Quest*, 1903; *Britain Across the Seas—Africa*

Junker, Wilhelm. *Travels in Africa 1882-1886*, 1892

Jameson, James S. *The Story of the Rear Column*, 1890

Krapf, J. Lewis. *Travels, Researches and Missionary Labours*, 1850

Lugard, F. D. *The Rise of our East African Empire*, 1893

Livingstone, David. *Missionary Travels and Researches*, 1857; *The Last Journals*, 1874

Lloyd, A. B. *In Dwarf Land and Cannibal Country*, 1899

Mackay, J. W. H. *The Story of the Life of Mackay of Uganda*, 1891

Moorehead, Alan. *The White Nile*, 1960; *The Blue Nile*, 1962

Murjebi. *Unpublished letters and papers belonging to the Murjebi family*

Newman, H. S. *Banani: The Transition from Slavery to Freedom in Zanzibar and Pemba*, 1898

Oliver, Roland. *The Missionary Factor in East Africa*, 1952

Oxford, U. P. *History of East Africa*, Vols. I & II

Owen, W. F. W. *Narrative of Voyages to Explore the Shores of Africa, Arabia, and Madagascar*, 1833

Peters, Carl. *New Light on Dark Africa*, 1891

Russell, C. E. B. *General Rigby, Zanzibar and the Slave Trade*, 1935

Speke, J. H. *What Led to the Discovery of the Source of the Nile*, 1864; *Journal of the Discovery of the Source of the Nile*, 1863

Stanley, H. M. *How I found Livingstone*, 1872; *Through the Dark Continent*, 1879; *The Congo and the Founding of the Free State*, 1885; *In Darkest Africa*, 1890; *My Kalulu, Prince, King and Slave*, 1890

Stanley's Despatches to the New York Herald 1871-1872, 1874-1877, Norman R. Bennet Editor, 1970

Stanley and Africa, 1890

The Autobiography of Sir Henry Morton Stanley, G.C.B., 1909, Edited by his wife Dorothy Stanley

Swann, A. J. *Fighting the Slave Hunters in Central Africa*, 1890

Sulivan, G. L. *Dhow Chasing in Zanzibar Waters*, 1873

Stevens, Thomas. *Scouting for Stanley in East Africa*, 1890

Schweinfurth, G. *Emin Pasha in Central Africa*, 1888

Stigand, C. H. *The Land of Zinj*, 1913

Thomson, Joseph. *To the Central African Lakes and Back*, 1879

Troup, J. R. *Stanley's Rear Column*, 1890

Tanganyika. *Notes and Records*

Tippu Tip. *Maisha ya Hamed bin Muhammed el Murjebi, yaani Tippu Tip*. Edited by Prof. Brode, 1903

Wauters, A. J. *Stanley's Emin Pasha Expedition*, 1890

Wissman, Hermann von *Through Equatorial Africa. My second Journey Through Equatorial Africa*, 1891

Werner, J. R. *A Visit to Stanley's Rear-Guard at Major Barttelot's Camp*, 1888

Zanzibar. *Reports from 1870 to 1905*

Index

161

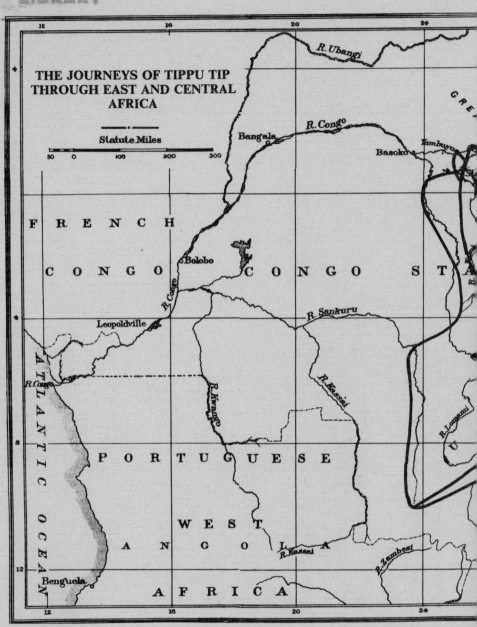

THE JOURNEYS OF TIPPU TIP THROUGH EAST AND CENTRAL AFRICA

Statute Miles

50   0   100   200   300

R. Ubangi

R. Congo

Bangala

Basoko

Yambuya

GREAT

F R E N C H

C O N G O

o Bolobo

R. Congo

C O N G O   S T A

Leopoldville

R. Sankuru

R. Kassai

R. Lomami

R. Congo

R. Kwango

A T L A N T I C   O C E A N

P O R T U G U E S E

U

W E S T

A N G O L A

R. Kassai

R. Zambesi

Benguela

A F R I C A